T0328688

Cambridge Elements

Elements in Child Development
edited by
Marc H. Bornstein
Eunice Kennedy Shriver National Institute of Child Health and Human Development, Bethesda
Institute for Fiscal Studies, London
UNICEF, New York City

CHILDREN'S EYEWITNESS TESTIMONY AND EVENT MEMORY

Martha E. Arterberry
Colby College

CAMBRIDGE
UNIVERSITY PRESS

University Printing House, Cambridge CB2 8BS, United Kingdom

One Liberty Plaza, 20th Floor, New York, NY 10006, USA

477 Williamstown Road, Port Melbourne, VIC 3207, Australia

314–321, 3rd Floor, Plot 3, Splendor Forum, Jasola District Centre,
New Delhi – 110025, India

103 Penang Road, #05–06/07, Visioncrest Commercial, Singapore 238467

Cambridge University Press is part of the University of Cambridge.

It furthers the University's mission by disseminating knowledge in the pursuit of
education, learning, and research at the highest international levels of excellence.

www.cambridge.org
Information on this title: www.cambridge.org/9781009124379
DOI: 10.1017/9781009128216

First published 2022

A catalogue record for this publication is available from the British Library.

ISBN 978-1-009-12437-9 Paperback
ISSN 2632-9948 (online)
ISSN 2632-993X (print)

Children's Eyewitness Testimony and Event Memory

Elements in Child Development

DOI: 10.1017/9781009128216
First published online: June 2022

Martha E. Arterberry
Colby College

Author for correspondence: Martha E. Arterberry, Martha.Arterberry@colby.edu

Abstract: This Element addresses the factors that influence children's accuracy in reporting on events and draws implications for children's ability to serve as reliable eyewitnesses. The following topics are covered: short- and long-term memory for event details; memory for stressful events; memory for the temporal order of events; memory for the spatial location of events; the ways poorly worded questions or intervening events interfere with memory; and individual differences in language development, understanding right from wrong and emotions, and cognitive processes. In addition, this Element considers how potential jurors perceive children as eyewitnesses and how the findings of the research on children's event memory inform best practices for interviewing children.

This Element also has a video abstract: www.cambridge.org/ChildDevelopment_Arterberry_abstract

Keywords: children's eyewitness testimony, event memory, suggestibility, cognitive development, jurors' perceptions

ISBNs: 9781009124379 (PB), 9781009128216 (OC)
ISSNs: 2632-9948 (online), 2632-993X (print)

Contents

Preface

My interest in eyewitness testimony began when I read Elizabeth Loftus' (1979) book titled *Eyewitness Testimony*. This reading was the culminating assignment for a course I took on learning and memory in fall 1981, taught by Professor Deborah Burke at Pomona College. I was fascinated. Seeing the application of all that I had learned that semester in Loftus' book highlighted the importance of basic research and how findings are translated to real-world contexts.

Then I was robbed. Over the winter break in early January 1982, I worked as a bank teller. A man approached my window, and he asked for all of the money in my drawer. As a seasoned bank teller, I enacted the protocol for such a situation. When he left the building, I went to a quiet place and wrote down everything I could remember. Over the next few hours, numerous law enforcement officers interviewed me. As I was answering questions, I (internally) analyzed their questioning practices: Were they (unintentionally) misleading me? Was my memory of the event being affected by telling and retelling what happened? The one question I still remember today is, "What color was the man's hat?" Hum … did he even have a hat? I could not remember the color, and I still question whether or not he was wearing a hat.

Fast forward to today. As a developmental scientist, I find the topic of children's eyewitness testimony, and more generally the questions pertaining to children's event memory, fascinating for the same reasons I loved Loftus' book. This topic has important real-world implications. Moreover, the topic is complex, and thus motivates study of a host of developmental areas and processes. Now my students at Colby College join me as I dive into these areas, and we conduct research on children's event memory that may have implications for eyewitness testimony. As we have learned and as you will see as you read this Element, complex questions do not have simple answers, but I hope you enjoy the journey.

1 Introduction

At what age can children be reliable eyewitnesses? This question has important practical implications because, unfortunately, children are witnesses to crimes, either directly or indirectly. Moreover, for some crimes, such as child physical or sexual abuse, the survivor may be the only witness. Figure 1 shows the different types of crimes involving children aged two to seventeen years living in the contiguous United States. Although these data were published in 2005 by Finkelhor et al., it is likely that the relative trends, if not the absolute numbers, apply to the present day. Even though much of the work on eyewitness testimony focuses on the situation of child sexual abuse, other crimes directly

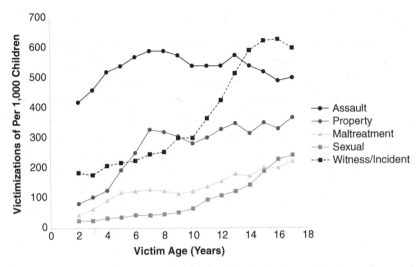

Figure 1 Crime involvement as victims or bystanders as a function of type of crime and age for children in the United States.

Note: Figure reproduced by M. E. Arterberry from Finkelhor et al. (2005) with permission.

involve children, including physical assault (the most common type of crime) and property violations. Moreover, about one in three children witness violent crimes or experience indirect victimization. Outside of criminal contexts, children report on events all the time. When parents or teachers encounter two or more children fighting, crying, or something broken, the first thing they ask is, "What happened?" Moreover, parents may ask what happened at school, peers may ask what someone ate for breakfast, grandparents may ask what they did first on a field trip, or siblings or peers may compare notes on a recent dental visit or a birthday party. All of these contexts involve memory for events.

The answer to the question about at what age children can be reliable eyewitnesses is elusive. For one reason, adults are not very reliable eyewitnesses (Loftus, 2019). Thus, how can children be expected to be reliable? Perhaps a more useful question is: What factors influence children's accuracy in reporting on events? Through exploring these factors, age trends may be identified, but it is unlikely that there is one age after which children are considered to be reliable. The question focusing on factors also moves the discussion to many aspects of episodic or event memory, not just those that pertain to criminal proceedings. Yes, eyewitness testimony and its accuracy are important, but recalling and reporting on events is a part of all children's everyday interactions.

What does it mean for a witness or for memory to be reliable? From a researcher's standpoint, reliability is a central concept. Researchers want their findings to be reliable in that they reflect truth, such as truth about principles (e.g., gravity) or truth in accurately characterizing behaviors (e.g., ways to attract someone's attention). Consequently, there are a number of procedures researchers follow, along with controls, to ensure that their results mean what they hope they mean. One test of a reliable study is doing it again and see if the same findings emerge. Replication of the same procedure by the same researchers is one way to do this. Alternatively, others may try to replicate the procedure. And still others may extrapolate from the original finding, reasoning that if it is true, then something else should be true. When talking about reliable memory of events, truth is also at stake. Memory should reflect what happened. Moreover, if someone is asked multiple times about the same event or if multiple people are asked about the same event, the details should be the same. When these conditions are met, memory is reliable.

1.1 Information-Processing Framework

Trying to determine the factors that influence children's accuracy in reporting on events has led to many discoveries about children's cognition, and this Element focuses on these discoveries, particularly on the development of event memory. Much of the research conducted on this topic comes from an information-processing framework (Atkinson & Shiffrin, 1968; Howe, 2015; Miller, 2002). The information-processing framework emerged in the 1960s and uses a computer metaphor for cognitive processes, particularly memory. The basic idea is that information is taken in, it is processed, it may be stored, it may be retrieved at a later date, and all of this is in service of behavior or an output. The framework has three key components – sensory register, short-term/working memory, and long-term memory – and three key processes – attention, encoding, and retrieval (see Figure 2). To illustrate this model, consider a vignette used by Smetana and Ball (2018, p. 2263) in

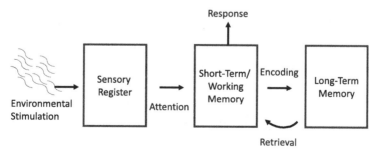

Figure 2 Schematic representation of the information-processing framework, after Atkinson & Shiffrin (1968) (created by M. E. Arterberry).

a study on moral transgressions: "One day, Madison and Sarah both decided to go play on the swings. Sarah was about to take a turn, but Madison shoved her so that she fell over, and Madison got on the swing."

All information processing begins with input, and in this model, input is defined as environmental stimulation. This stimulation – whether wavelengths of light, sound frequencies, pressure, temperature, or chemical properties – enters the system via the sensory register. A bystander witnessing the swing event described previously would be awash in energy impinging on the senses (such as the color of the children's clothing, their faces, their movements, the sound of the swing, the change in air as the swing moves, the feel of wood chips under the feet, the children's voices or screams, and the sunshine). Some of this information is central to the event (the actor's faces and movements), and some is peripheral (the wood chips). This information is collected for a brief time in the sensory register. The sensory register has a large capacity but a very short duration. Thus, much of this information disappears quickly. The information that does not disappear has been moved to short-term memory/working memory via attentional processes. Attention is selective in that there are limits to how much information can be attended to at one time. Often the most salient features capture attention (e.g., bright colors, flashing lights, and movement).

Information that is in conscious awareness, or attended to, is in short-term/working memory. Short-term/working memory has a small capacity and a short duration. Adults hold about five to nine (or seven plus or minus two) items in short-term memory (Miller, 1956), and as long as the information is being used, it remains active or accessible. For example, a bystander may be surprised by the pushing event in the swing vignette and continue to watch Madison on the swing, allowing for more opportunities to remember what she looked like, the clothes she was wearing, and the like. Information that is saved for later is encoded and stored in long-term memory. Long-term memory has an infinite capacity and long duration. The bystander may evaluate the shoving as a moral transgression and decide to tell a teacher after recess is over or a parent once home from the playground. With this goal in mind, details about the event may be stored in long-term memory. Later, information from long-term memory can be retrieved and moved back to short-term/working memory. Successful retrieval relies on effective encoding. Encoding processes vary, but those that allow for deeper encoding, such as extracting the meaning of the information and storing it with information already known, increase the chance of successful retrieval. For example, the bystander may encode the present event by tying it to their memories of other transgressions, perhaps previous acts committed by Madison or other instances where children shoved one another. Retrieval cues help with retrieval, such as remembering the event that took place on the playground or someone asking why Sarah was upset.

Retrieving information from memory involves one of two processes – recall and recognition. The term recall often refers to the general process of pulling something from memory. However, recall in the information-processing framework is specific to retrieval without outside support. For example, the statement "tell me what happened" cues open-ended recall. The respondent does just that – tells what they can remember – without any guidance by the interviewer. Cued recall provides a little more support in that questions provide context. An example question might be, "Tell me how Sarah fell down?" Another type of retrieval is recognition. With recognition, the interviewer is asking for the selection of a response, such as "Did Madison shove Sarah?" (yes/no) or "What color was her shirt? Blue or green?" Recognition is easier than recall because with recognition the respondent is provided with more context than with recall and may only need to confirm or deny the information.

Whereas the information-processing framework is useful for organizing knowledge about and understanding the processes involved in event memory, reliable event memory is not just about attention, encoding, storage, and retrieval. There are other factors, including factors pertaining to the context, both internal (e.g., stress) and external (e.g., salience of the event) and factors pertaining to individuals (e.g., language skills) that intersect with memory for events and children's ability to report on them. To explore the topic of event memory and its implications for eyewitness testimony, research from other theoretical perspectives, including attachment theory and sociocultural theory, is included.

1.2 Overview

This Element begins by identifying a number of topics that enlighten understanding of children's event memory. Next, the Element considers one study in detail to understand the role of knowledge on short- and long-term memory of event details and to illustrate typical methodology used to study event memory. Following this study, the following topics are considered: memory for stressful events, children's ability to remember the temporal order of events and the spatial location of where events occurred, and the ways poorly worded questions and/or intervening events (such as conversations about the event) may interfere with accurate reporting. Following an understanding of children's memory performance under ideal and nonideal conditions, the Element considers the ways that children differ in the areas of language development, understanding right from wrong and emotions, and cognitive processes and how these differences predict better (or worse) event memory. Finally, the Element turns to how potential jurors perceive children as eyewitnesses and how the findings of the research on children's event memory inform the best practices for interviewing children in criminal contexts. Because a number of researchers are interested in the lower age limits for when children can accurately report verbally on events, much of the research herein focuses on children between three and eight years of age.

2 Many Factors and One Comprehensive Study

2.1 Concept Map

When considering the factors that influence children's accuracy in reporting on events, clearly memory development is important. But, so is understanding other aspects of cognitive development, individual differences, and context. Figure 3 is one way to diagram the various topics that place eyewitness testimony in a larger context. This concept map is in no way complete, but it illustrates the complexity of this topic and the way that subareas intersect with the central question regarding the factors that influence children's memory reliability.

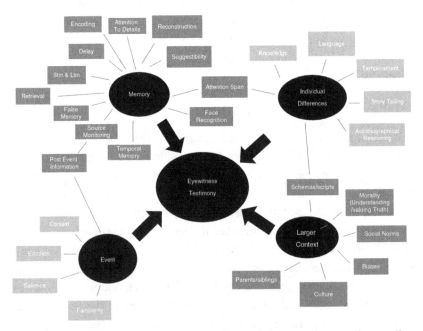

Figure 3 Schematic representation of topic areas that pertain to understanding of children's eyewitness testimony (created by M. E. Arterberry).

As is the case with much of the research in psychology, there is a trade-off between naturalistic studies (or ecologically valid studies) and those with a high level of control (often laboratory studies). In the research reviewed here, there is a balance between realistic contexts and experimental control. This trade-off may appear more acute here than in other areas of psychological research because of the field's interest in application. If a case relied on the testimony of a child witness, all parties involved would want to know whether or not the child witness is developmentally ready for such a task. Is this assessment best done under controlled laboratory conditions or in the messy real-world? Both approaches, controlled laboratory and real-world, provide a rich understanding of children's event memory. The next subsection begins by describing one study that addresses several of the topics included in the concept map, and the study illustrates how researchers can use a real event and a realistic questioning context without losing experimental control.

2.2 Short- and Long-Term Memory of an Event

Ornstein et al. (2006) were not the first researchers to explore children's event memory; however, over the years, they made significant contributions to the field's understanding of this topic. Their study conducted in 2006 is particularly ambitious and informative and so merits description in considerable detail for several reasons. First, it serves as an illustration of how this type of research is done with children, including the many considerations when designing a study that yields interpretable findings. To this end, some of the methodological decisions the researchers made as they designed and executed the study are highlighted. Second, the study serves as a model for many experiments that were done afterward to address children's event memory. Thus, later descriptions of studies can be brief, given this foundation. Finally, the findings serve as a comparison to those of other studies presented later in this Element.

For the context, Ornstein et al. (2006) took advantage of a naturally occurring event that all children in the United States (hopefully) experience – an annual well-child medical visit. This visit includes a (ideally) standard set of medical assessments regardless of medical provider. Moreover, the visit is intimate. A stranger (nurse or doctor) touches the children, such as when they place a stethoscope on their chest to listen to their heart and lungs, and the children may be partially undressed. For most children, this visit is not stressful, outside of the typical wariness children might have for medical settings (it is at these visits that children may receive inoculations). This context is especially useful for understanding children's event memory with the goal of drawing implications for eyewitness testimony because this medical context is like the contexts in which children find themselves victims of crime, most notably those involving abuse. Often abuse events are repeated, involve some type of physical contact, and are perpetrated by a trusted adult.

In this work, Ornstein et al. (2006) addressed four questions. First, they asked how memory for the event changed between four and seven years of age. Second, they asked how long children retained information about a specific well-child visit, and third, they asked whether repeated questioning sustained or reactivated memory of the event. Finally, they asked how children's previous knowledge of an event contributed to their memory of the event. In other words, do children who know more about what typically happens in well-child pediatric visits remember more about the events that occurred during a specific visit than children who know less?

To answer these questions, they recruited families with children aged four, five, six, and seven years as they approached their children's well-child pediatric visit. Before the visit, a researcher interviewed half of the children in their home and asked them what typically happens at these visits. Within a month of the knowledge interview, all of the children experienced the well-child visit, and a parent used a checklist to indicate which of nineteen procedures the child experienced. Next, immediately after the visit, all children were interviewed by a researcher about the visit. Three months later, researchers interviewed half of the children again, and then six months later, researchers interviewed all of the children about the visit. See Figure 4.

The interview about the event was hierarchical in that first open-ended questions probed for what children remembered ("Tell me what happened at your checkup"). Then yes/no questions probed for details about specific events

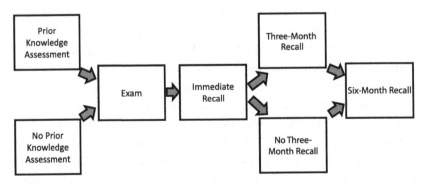

Figure 4 Procedural timeline for the interviews and the well-child exam experienced by children in Ornstein et al. (2006).

Note: Figure created by M. E. Arterberry using information in Table 1 in Ornstein et al. (2006).

not mentioned during the open-ended phase ("Did the nurse find out if you can hear ok?"). In addition, when necessary, children were prompted to elaborate ("Tell me how she did that"). Next, the researchers asked two leading questions for each medical feature, one leading to the correct answer and one leading to the incorrect answer. Finally, the researchers asked eight yes/no extra-event questions that probed for activities that might occur during a medical visit but not at a well-child visit, such as wrapping one's leg in a bandage.

2.2.1 A Methodological Aside

Those unfamiliar with research in psychology or research with children may not fully appreciate the number of decisions Ornstein et al. (2006) made when designing and implementing this research project. There are a number of decisions that make this a strong investigation. First, they asked only half of the children about their knowledge of the visit. From this baseline assessment, the investigators were able to determine generally what children know about well-child visits at the four ages (i.e., four to seven years). But the investigators also were able to determine whether children who were asked in the month preceding a visit about such visits showed greater memory for the specific experience compared with children who were not asked. It is possible that children remembered more about the actual visit because they were asked in advance about it. In other words, the knowledge interview asked children to retrieve information about such visits, and that may have made them pay more attention during the actual visit, or it may have allowed them to store new information about the visit along with past information more readily than children who did not have the opportunity to retrieve their knowledge about well-child visits. Ornstein et al. (2006) also asked only half of the children questions at three months. This decision allowed them to test whether questioning at three months enhanced memory at six months after the event. The children who were not asked questions at three months served as an important control. Another control assessed children's language abilities. Because the children were required to describe what they experienced and also answer specific questions about the medical encounter, the researchers wanted to be sure they were measuring memory for the event rather than children's ability to talk about it.

Other important decisions were made when considering how to implement the procedure. The children were recruited from two pediatric groups, and six pediatricians and five nurses provided care across the sample. In practice, providers sometimes skip one or more of the standard assessments in their implementation of the well-child visit. To account for this variability across visits, parents completed a checklist during the exam so that the researchers knew which of the possible nineteen components of the exam were provided (the average was fourteen to fifteen components across all four age groups), and thus the researchers were able to tailor their questioning and scoring to items that were experienced or not.

The hierarchical questioning during the interviews is also an important methodological decision because it allowed the researchers to compare recall and recognition. The researchers first asked children to tell them what happened, using open-ended prompts to facilitate recall. The first prompt was "Tell me what happened during your checkup" (Ornstein et al., 2006, p. 335). Then children were asked more specific open-ended questions like "Tell me what the nurse/doctor does/did to check you." This type of prompting allowed children to report what they could remember without any assistance or cuing from the interviewer. This type of memory is called recall. After children indicated they did not remember anything more, they were asked direct questions that were increasingly specific to assess recognition. For example, if children did not mention the hearing test, they were asked, "Did the nurse find out if you can hear okay?" If children answered yes, the researchers followed with a request for more information, such as "How did the nurse do that?" Some of the direct questions were not misleading ("Did you put on earphones and listen to sounds?"), whereas others were about events that did occur (hearing test) but provided incorrect information ("Did the nurse whisper into your ear?").

2.2.2 Now for Some Results

At the immediate interview, the amount of details recalled increased with child age, ranging from 68 percent for four-year-olds to 88 percent for seven-year-olds. This increase was most apparent for the open-ended questions (Figure 5). Not surprisingly, rates of recall went down after three months, with children recalling 55 percent to 74 percent of the details four and seven years of age, respectively (Figure 5). Performance on the open-ended questions did not significantly drop between three and six months (Figure 5). Despite age differences for information recalled at each time point, the rates of forgetting were equal across ages, with children forgetting approximately 18 percent of the details by three months after the event. Children were also remarkably consistent in resisting the questions about events that did not happen, with denials ranging between 75 and 96 percent across the three assessments.

Ornstein et al. (2006) also found differences across the four ages in terms of children's knowledge of what typically happens at a well-child visit. Moreover,

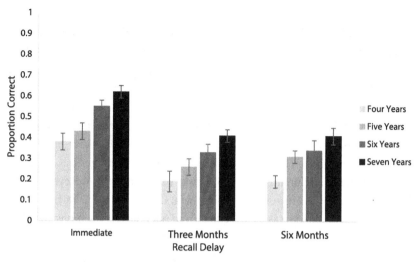

Figure 5 Mean proportion correct recall as a function of child age and interview timing from Ornstein et al. (2006).
Note: Figure created by M. E. Arterberry using data provided in Table 3 in Ornstein et al. (2006). Error bars indicate standard error.

knowledge correlated with immediate open-ended recall, but not with performance three and six months after the pediatric visit. Thus, the more knowledge children had about an event that was about to happen, the more they remembered the details of the specific event, at least when questioned immediately afterward. At the same time, knowledge scores and forgetting rates showed no relation, such that knowledge did not preserve memories after a delay of at least three months. Once forgetting happened in this study, there was no way to reverse it. Repeated questioning at three months did not affect performance on the open-ended questions at six months (performance remained low) or on correct denials of the questions probing for extra-event activities (performance remained high).

2.2.3 Comparisons to Other Research

The results from this study converge with many other studies by showing that older children remembered more than younger children. This age difference is the one constant finding across most of the studies in children's event memory, to the point that studies that do not find age differences, or find a developmental reversal (such that younger children do better than older children), tell us more about event memory than studies that do show age differences. Two examples of a lack of age differences come from the present study. First, children of all ages accurately rejected questions probing for extra-event activities. In other words, even the youngest children were highly accurate in denying events that did not happen, a finding also found by Baker-Ward et al. (1993) and Principe et al. (2000), who also tested children's memory for a pediatric visit. Second, even though the older children remembered more details than the younger children, the rate of forgetting (18 percent of the information originally remembered) between immediate recall and three months after the event was consistent across all ages. This finding is surprising in that it does not fit other models of forgetting rates among children: Typically, older children forget less information than younger children in laboratory tasks (e.g., Brainerd & Reyna, 1995; Brainerd et al., 2012). However, consistent with Ornstein et al. (2006), Principe et al. (2000) also found rates of forgetting from open-ended questions asked of three- and five-year-olds to be in this range. In their study, 10–15 percent of the information was lost across twelve weeks. Being questioned six weeks after an event helped to reduce forgetting at twelve weeks (Principe et al., 2000), but being questioned at twelve weeks did not reduce forgetting at six months (Ornstein et al., 2006).

In Ornstein et al. (2006), memory for event details was high immediately after the event and then declined by three months with no further loss of information at six months. High performance immediately after an event is expected and has been found by others (e.g., Baker-Ward et al., 1993; Fivush et al., 1984; Klemfuss & Wang, 2017; Principe et al., 2000; Sutherland et al., 2003), as well as a decrease in memory after a delay (e.g., Klemfuss & Wang, 2017). But there are exceptions. For example, six months after a visit to a museum, 5.5-year-olds remembered as many details as they did immediately after the event, and they retained much of this information until one year later (Fivush et al., 1984). Similarly, memory of an injury serious enough to require a visit to an emergency department for treatment did not diminish over the years. Children who experienced the injury when they were between two and five years of age remembered the injury with high accuracy ten years later; however, memory for the in-hospital treatment declined, as early as two years after the experience (Peterson, 2015; Peterson et al., 2007).

Finally, Ornstein et al. (2006) showed how prior knowledge affected memory for event details. Children who reported more knowledge of pediatric exams in the month before their visit recalled more information after the visit. Prior knowledge often comes from experience; however, it can also come from being told what is going to happen. In Sutherland et al. (2003), teachers told a group of five- to seven-year-olds what was going to happen at an upcoming pirate visit. A second group of teachers engaged children in a general discussion about pirates, and a third group engaged in a neutral discussion the day before the visit. Children who were told specifically what was going to happened recalled more about the pirate visit five days later than the other two groups. Moreover, the children incorporated event-specific information into their general knowledge of pirates, when assessed fourteen days later. Thus, prior knowledge may enable better attention strategies to details and deeper encoding of events as they are ongoing such that the specific details are remembered better. At the same time, experiencing a specific event enhances knowledge about such events generally.

2.3 Summary

Ornstein et al.'s research using a real-world experience for U.S. children sets the stage for this Element by addressing some of the factors in Figure 3. They found that older children remembered more event details than younger children, memory decreased across a three-month delay, and event knowledge facilitated memory. Moreover, children of all ages accurately rejected questions about events that did not occur.

A strength of this ambitious study is that Ornstein et al. (2006) took advantage of a naturally occurring event – a pediatric visit that is predictable and standardized across providers – to study children's event memory. Moreover, the well-child checkup is intimate, such that one or more adults touch the children, aligning this event with events that children may be asked to testify about, namely: physical or sexual abuse. However, there are differences between a well-child checkup (or trips to a museum, or visits with a pirate at school) and criminal events, which call into question the extent to which Ornstein et al.'s findings may generalize. Three differences are (a) the stress level of the well-child visit compared to abusive events, (b) the frequency with which abusive events recurred, and (c) the delay periods (survivors often do not report abuse immediately after it occurs; Goodman et al., 2019). In addition, there is little control over what happened during the three- and six-month periods. Did children go to the doctor's office again for another reason (introducing new post-event details)? Did parents talk about the well-child visit, or did children compare notes with peers about their visits (allowing for rehearsal)? In short, whereas this one ambitious study ticks a number of the boxes in Figure 3, there are many more factors to consider.

3 Stressful Events

Despite the comprehensive nature of the study conducted by Ornstein et al. (2006), a number of outstanding questions are raised about what factors predict children's ability to report details of an event. This section focuses on children's memory for stressful or emotional events.

3.1 Emotional Stimuli and Events

The events that lead to real-world eyewitness testimony are likely stressful for children, and children differ in how they react to stressful events (Gunnar et al., 2015). How stress intersects with information processing is complicated, and there are no hard and fast rules about how stressful events or emotionally valenced stimuli affect memory for events. On the one hand, stressful events may be unusual and likely to garner attention due to their novelty, and thus may be remembered better. On the other hand, stressful events may result in too much arousal, thus interfering with attention and encoding. As a result, these events may be remembered less well than less stressful events.

A large literature on emotion and memory in adults leads to the general view that emotional stimuli are remembered better than neutral stimuli and that negatively valenced materials are remembered better than positively valenced materials (e.g., LaBar & Cabeza, 2006). Research conducted with children is not as straightforward. For example, in one study, children as young as five years of age rated negative images, such as a tarantula, as less pleasant than neutral images, and they rated positive images, such as a flower, as more pleasant than neutral images (Leventon et al., 2014). These same children showed differences in physical arousal and neurological measures for negative, neutral, and positive stimuli. Yet, there was no difference in recognition performance for the three types of stimuli. In contrast, using stories that presented negative, neutral, or positive themes, Van Bergen et al. (2015) found that five- and six-year-olds showed the expected adult pattern by recalling more details from emotional stories compared with neutral ones, and more details from negative stories than from positive ones (see also Alexander et al., 2010, for a similar finding for eight- to twelve-year-olds). However, Brainerd et al. (2010) showed that children's recognition memory was better for positive word lists (e.g., baby) compared with negative word lists (e.g., spider) and for high arousal lists (e.g., music) compared with low arousal lists (e.g., sleep). Not only do these studies provide conflicting findings, they also use highly controlled conditions. Real-world stressful contexts require children to manage their emotions while participating in, attending to, encoding, and storing (or not) details of the event.

To study children's memory for stressful and/or emotionally charged events in naturally occurring events, researchers often turn to the medical context, such as receiving inoculations, experiencing outpatient medical procedures (such as voiding cystourethrogram fluoroscopy – VCUG), and visits to the dentist or emergency department (Chae et al., 2014; Peterson et al., 2007; Quas et al., 1999). For example, Baker-Ward et al. (2015) assessed 4.5- to 11.5-year-old children's level of stress during a pediatric dental visit involving operative procedures (not preventative care). The researchers measured behavioral signs of stress exhibited by the children during the procedure, and then asked them to recall the details of the procedure within thirty minutes of it taking place. Surprisingly, the level of stress exhibited by the children did not predict memory for details. Instead, parent preparation in terms of conversation the night before and previous history with restorative dental procedures did predict memory for details in that the more preparation or previous history resulted in increased memory. Similarly, elaborative conversations with parents after a visit to the emergency department predicted children's short-term recall of the hospital visit (Peterson et al., 2007). Elaborative conversations involve encouraging children to elaborate on what the parent or child has said and encouraging the continuation of conversations (e.g., Hedrick et al., 2009). The use of *Wh*-questions contributes to elaborative conversations, such as by asking "What happened next?" and "Why do you think she did that?" In addition to the use of questions to encourage children to elaborate, parents who respond positively to comments and allow children to direct the conversations also support accurate memory at a later time (Van de Kaap-Deeder et al., 2020). Thus, children's memory for emotional events may depend on what else is going on, before, during, and/or after the event.

3.2 Parent–Child Attachment

Parents who prepare their children in advance for stressful experiences and/or engage their children in positive elaborative talk may be more sensitive to their children's needs than parents who do not (Salmon & Reese, 2015). This possibility moves us into the realm of attachment, a bit of a surprising topic in an Element on children's event memory. Attachment is an enduring relationship that develops in the first seven months or so of life, and it is built on a system of trust (Bowlby, 1969). Through their everyday interactions, infants signal their needs and parents and other caregivers respond appropriately (or not). Resulting from these interactions are attachment relationships, which are described as either secure (optimal) or insecure (Ainsworth & Wittig, 1969). This early relationship sets the stage for future interactions, serving as a template or schema for how relationships work (called the internal working model by Bowlby, 1958). Children who have secure attachments to their parents typically have parents who are sensitive and responsive to their needs (Holmes & Farnfield, 2014). Thus, elaborative talk may be a proxy for the way parents support their children (or not) when children face stressful situations. Alexander et al. (2002) suggested that attachment may affect memory for stressful events in at least three possible ways. First, securely attached children may have better coping strategies than insecure children. As a result, they may be better able to regulate their emotions during a stressful situation, perhaps allowing them to pay better attention to the details of the event compared to insecurely attached children. Second, storage of event details may be affected by attachment classification, especially if the events are consistent with a child's view of how relationships work. These relationship schemas may affect the extent to which memories for events are accurately stored or distorted depending on how well the events conform to the way the children expect relationships to work. This idea of an internal working model setting the stage for storage is similar to the way past knowledge appears to facilitate memory for events (Ornstein et al., 2006). Finally, attachment classification may affect retrieval or willingness to talk about events, whether remembered accurately or not. Securely attached children, again due to their ability to manage their emotions, may be more comfortable talking about distressing events from the past compared with insecurely attached children.

3.3 Summary

There is no clear answer regarding whether stressful or emotionally laden events are remembered better or worse than neutral events. Because children (and adults) react to stressful and emotional situations differently, other factors, such as the type of support children have before, during, and/or after events, also affect children's memory. The discussion of attachment raises the question of individual differences, which may be why it is hard to answer the general question about at what age children are able to be reliable eyewitnesses. The theme of individual is addressed later in Section 6.

4 Memory for When and Where

Up to this point, this Element focused on children's memory for event details (e.g., who did what to whom), with little attention paid to the ordering of the details or where the event occurred. These questions of temporal memory (when) and spatial memory (where) are also important features of events. They help place the individual components, such as a well-child visit, into a larger context, such as going to a new doctor's office three days after a birthday party. Questions of where and when, and how many times, are also important in legal contexts. As summarized by Wandry et al. (2012), when an event occurred has implications for statutes of limitations, or the maximum amount of time one may begin legal proceedings. Moreover, there are well-known cases, such as the Catholic Priest sexual abuse scandal, survivors did not come forward until many years later, complicating prosecution of the abusers due to unclear answers to questions of when and where abuse took place (Frawley-O'Dea & Goldner, 2007). Also, defendants are entitled to full knowledge of their charge, including when and where the alleged crime took place. From a defendant's perspective, temporal and spatial information are important for determining alibis.

4.1 Temporal Memory

The components of an event unfold in a temporal sequence. For example, at a well-child visit the doctor may listen to the child's heart *before* a hearing check. Being able to recall what happened and the order in which events happened, or particularizing events, is central to eyewitness reports (e.g., Powell et al., 2007). Temporal memory has been studied in a variety of ways, often by asking children about autobiographical events (Fivush, in press). For example, researchers asked children to recall how long ago an event occurred from the present (e.g., three months ago; Friedman & Lyon, 2005), or when one event occurred in relation to another (e.g., trip to a zoo versus first plane ride; Pathman, Larkina et al., 2013). These types of questions posed difficulty for children as young as three to four years of age. In contrast, six- to eight-year-olds were able to order events, such as which happened before another (Pathman, Doydum, & Bauer, 2013). Yet, when asked to order salient events, such as Christmas, Easter, birthday, and the Fourth of July, eight- and nine-year-olds were unable to judge which pairs of events, such as Christmas or their birthday, was longer ago (Friedman, 1992; Friedman et al., 1995). Similarly, when asked to place events from one day along a timeline, seven- and eight-year-olds placed events within 10 percent of their parents' estimates; however, five- and six-year-olds' estimation errors were twice as large, and four-year-olds' estimation errors were three times as large as those of seven- to eight-year-old children (Gosse & Roberts, 2014).

Many autobiographical events are repeated and often discussed (e.g., a birthday happens every year). What about memory for events that are novel or never experienced before? Temporal ordering of nonrecurring events, such as an experience at a zoo, or the order of events in a storybook, is difficult for young children. When questioned about the order of events in a relatively short period (either immediately or within a day), three- to five-year-olds correctly ordered 50–60 percent of the events (Arterberry & Albright, 2020; Deker & Pathman, 2021). Performance increased to about 80 percent by eight- to ten-year-olds.

When asked about nontemporal details, three- to four-year-olds remembered 87 percent of the event details.

Why is reporting on the temporal order of events (what happened when) more difficult than other event details (such as the specific activities)? One possibility is that reporting about the temporal order of events requires the use of temporal terms, such as *before* and *after*. For example, when asked "Did the nurse listen to your heart before checking your hearing?", children need to understand the meaning of *before*. Additionally, in their retelling of events, they need to be able to produce temporal terms. By three years of age, 59 percent of children produce *before* and 84 percent produce *after*. Use of *before* and *after* increases to 97 percent and 100 percent, respectively, by five years of age (Busby Grant & Suddendorf, 2009). Despite the fact that children produced the terms *before* and *after* on a regular basis, they were less accurate in how they used these terms. Similarly, Tillman and Barner (2015) noted that children use time words, such as *minute* and *hour*, early in development, but they take years to acquire an understanding of their precise meanings. However, in tasks where children do not have to use language, such as ordering events along a timeline or retrieving objects in a hide-and-seek game, temporal memory does not improve (Arterberry & Albright, 2020; Hayne & Imuta, 2011; Scarf et al., 2017).

A second possibility is that children's ability to recall the temporal order of events may be related to executive function. Executive function is a general term describing the mental processes that allow us to plan, pay attention, and do multiple tasks successfully (Muller & Kerns, 2015). Some tasks require inaction, such as inhibiting a response in the "Simon Says" game. Other tasks require consideration of multiple rules or options and decide the best course of action. These processes are involved when focusing on one task, such as looking up a number on a cellphone, and when engaging in more than one task at a time (having a conversation with someone and walking down the street, while trying to look up a phone number). Executive functions increase with age, and they are correlated with improved performance in a number of domains (Zelazo & Muller, 2011). One executive function is cognitive flexibility, and it can be measured using the Dimensional Change Card Sort (DCCS) Task (Zelazo et al., 1996). The task includes ten cards depicting blue or yellow flowers and ten cards depicting blue and yellow trucks. Children are first taught to sort by one dimension, such as shape ("Put all the flowers here and all the trucks there."). After they have sorted all twenty cards, researchers then ask them to sort by the other dimension, such as color ("Put all the yellow ones here and all the blue ones there."). Children with more cognitive flexibility are able to shift from sorting using one dimension to sorting using another dimension.

Arterberry and Albright (2020) showed that children's cognitive flexibility predicted memory for the temporal ordering of events in a storybook, such that children with greater cognitive flexibility showed better temporal memory. This prediction held beyond age. In other words, the age of the children (between three and six years) did not predict how well they did in remembering the order of events in a storybook. Instead, children who had more cognitive flexibility showed higher temporal memory accuracy than those who showed less cognitive flexibility. The complexity of a temporal memory task may be analogous to seeing a card with both a shape and a color, and to remember which rule to use for a correct response, as in the DCCS task. Being able to consider what happened before versus after in the storybook involves the consideration of two events at a time and evaluating the correct answer.

The DCCS task measures more than one executive function. It includes inhibition (e.g., children need to inhibit the previous rule), working memory (e.g., children need to remember the current rule), and attentional control (e.g., children need to focus on the relevant feature of the stimulus). Children vary in how well they can engage these executive functions, and it is likely that children who are more successful are more advanced cognitively than those who have difficulty. Indeed, other researchers show that executive functions predicted recall of temporal and contextual information in four- to sixteen-year-olds, likely reflecting maturation of underlying cortical areas (e.g., Cycowicz et al., 2001; Picard et al., 2012).

For many assessments of memory, delay from the time of the event to when one is asked to report on the event is important. Recall that in Ornstein et al. (2006; Figure 5), children aged four to seven years lost about 18 percent of the details within three months of a well-child visit. When studying children's memory for the temporal ordering of events, delay between the two events is also an important variable. Adults, and children by age eight, show a temporal distance effect or lag effect, which refers to the fact that the greater the temporal distance between the two events, the higher the accuracy in determining their temporal order (Deker & Pathman, 2021; Pathman, Doydum, & Bauer, 2013; Pathman, Larkina et al., 2013). Deker and Pathman (2021) studied children attending a weeklong zoo camp. Each day the children engaged in a set of activities in one area of the zoo, and the staff kept track of who did what where. On the last day of the camp, the experimenters questioned the children about events that happened one day apart (called short lag) and events that happened three days apart (called long lag). In addition, the experimenters asked children about the ordering of two events on the same last day. Deker and Pathman (2021) found that four- to five-year-olds did not show the lag effect, or better temporal memory, for events separated by three days compared with one day

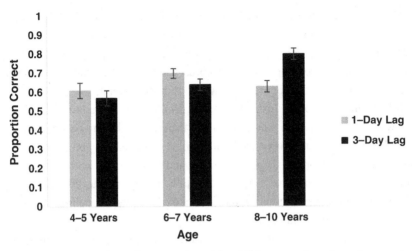

Figure 6 Temporal details remembered by children as a function of age and whether the two details occurred within one day of each other (short lag) or separated across three days (long lag).

Note: Figure reproduced by M. E. Arterberry from Figure 1 in Deker and Pathman (2021) with permission. Error bars indicate standard error.

(Figure 6). Moreover, their memory for the ordering of the events was poor and the findings suggest that they were guessing. Six- and seven-year-olds were significantly above chance (65–79 percent correct), but their memory for the short- and long-lag events was not different (Figure 6). It was not until eight to ten years of age that children showed the lag effect by answering more questions correctly about which of two events happened first when there was a three-day lag between the two events versus a one-day lag between the events (Figure 6). Finally, all three age groups had trouble ordering events that occurred on the same day.

Thus, children's memory for temporal information is protracted compared to memory for other aspects of events, such as the actual activities (e.g., Arterberry & Albright, 2020; Friedman, 2014). Children at least by the age of three form autobiographical memories, and they can report what typically happens in familiar events. However, recalling when events occur in relation to other events, such as visiting the giraffe before or after feeding a cheetah, or whether one's birthday occurred before or after Christmas, is difficult. Young children's experience may be like a "jumbled box of snapshots" (Friedman, 1993, p. 44), in which they have a store of details that are not temporally connected to one another. One factor supporting the development of temporal memory may be executive function, as indexed by cognitive flexibility, a finding that implicates neurological maturation. A network of regions including the medial temporal lobe and the prefrontal cortex may support temporal memory (Pathman & Ghetti, 2014), and these regions govern executive functions (Cycowicz et al., 2001).

4.2 Spatial Memory

Knowing what happened when is one piece of event information. Knowing what happened where is another. Memory for the spatial location of events is also important for fully reporting on events. Fewer studies have looked at children's memory for event location compared to temporal information, and it is unclear how accurate spatial memory is. For example, Peterson et al. (2007) found that children aged two to five years encoded location information in personally experienced events, such as where they were when they broke their arm several years after the event. In contrast, Pillemer et al. (1994) found that three- to four-year-old children could not remember where they were when they heard a fire alarm resulting from popcorn burning in their school. Two weeks later, 94 percent of the four-year-olds said that they were on the playground when they heard the alarm, but actually they were in the classroom (they were later evacuated to the playground). Moreover, few children recalled the cause of the fire. Other researchers also show that memory for location or context is generally less accurate than memory for other event details, such as the activities that took place in that location. For example, four- and six-year-olds remembered items that they played with an hour ago with close to 100 percent accuracy, but they had difficulty reporting (40 percent correct) in which of two rooms they played with the items (Ngo et al., 2017). Comparing immediate recall with recall after a one-week delay, Bauer et al. (2016) showed that four-year-olds remember location information; however, it was still not as accurate as memory for the activities done at each location. In their study, children completed four activities at four locations. At both immediate and one-week delay interviews, children showed higher recall for activities than for locations (Figure 7). As shown in Figure 7, remembering both the activities and the location (or the conjunction of activity and location) was more difficult than remembering only the activity, or only the location. Improvement in memory for location increases with age across four to eight years (Bauer et al., 2012).

Remembering where an event took place in addition to what happened, or features of the people or objects involved in the event, requires a binding of the relations among the stimuli. In other words, the individual components of the event (person's face, activities, and location) are combined to form one memory

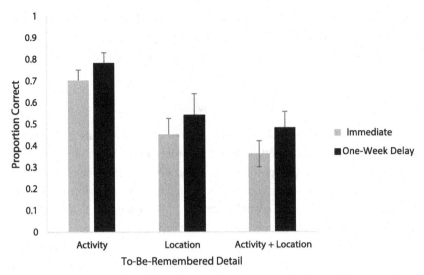

Figure 7 Four-year-old children's proportion correct cued recall for what they did (Activity) where (Location) immediately after experiencing four events and after a one-week delay. The apparent increase in memory one week later was not statistically significant.

Note: Figure reproduced by M. E. Arterberry from Figure 2a in Bauer et al. (2016) with permission. Values converted to proportion correct from number correct. Error bars indicate standard error.

rather than encoding the components separately (e.g., one memory of a face, one memory of an activity, and one memory of a location). This process takes place at encoding, and it develops across the first years of life (Sluzenski et al., 2006). Six-year-olds show better performance on tasks requiring memory binding than younger children (Newcombe et al., 2014; Ngo et al., 2017; Sluzenski et al., 2006), and confusion results when different events or objects are shown in the same contexts, or the same events or objects are shown in different contexts (Benear et al., 2021).

4.3 Summary

Both where and when an event occurred in addition to the activities engaged in are important components of event memory. Compared to temporal memory, memory for location is easier for young children to report, but accuracy still lags behind reporting on nonspatial features of objects or events. Extending these findings to an eyewitness context, interrogators may need to rely on children's reports of what happened and not expect them to remember what happened when or where.

5 Reporting on Events Under Nonideal Conditions

To this point, this Element has considered research in which children experienced events and were questioned either immediately or at a later time. Researchers took care not to mislead the children with the wording of the questions or interfering with children's memory of the events in other ways. As an example, Ornstein et al. (2006) took pictures of the children holding a balloon after their well-child visit to use as a reminder about which pediatric visit the researchers were interested in when they questioned the children three or six months later in case children visited the same doctor in the intervening time for another medical reason. Ornstein et al. (2006) also asked open-ended questions first so that the children could report all that they remembered before being asked questions that probed for specific details ("Did the nurse test your hearing?"). Moreover, most of the questions were direct rather than misleading ("Did nurse test your hearing by whispering into your ear?" – the answer is no). Under ideal conditions, children remembered event details accurately, and they were unlikely to agree to events that did not happen, such as being asked whether the doctor or nurse wrapped the child's leg in a bandage.

   Not all real-world or experimental situations are ideal. This Element now turns to contexts that result in less accurate reporting by children, including when misleading questions are asked, when children are pressured to agree to what the interviewer suggests, and when incorrect post-event information is present. The larger term for when children are impacted by these and other factors is suggestibility. Suggestibility is defined as "the degree to which children's encoding, storage, retrieval, and reporting of events can be influenced by a range of social and psychological factors" (Ceci & Bruck, 1993, p. 404). This definition is broad, and there are many ways to interfere with witnesses' accuracy, either intentionally or unintentionally.

5.1 The Way Witnesses Are Questioned

A primary source of suggestibility is misleading questions, and in real-world situations interviewers may not even be aware that they are asking misleading questions. A classic demonstration of how the wording of questions can lead to inaccurate testimony is a study conducted by Loftus and Palmer (1974). They showed college-aged participants videos of cars in accidents. Right after the video, the researchers asked participants to report how fast the two cars were going when they *smashed* into each other versus *hit* each other. A week later, participants reported the speed of the cars and whether they remembered seeing glass at the scene (there was none). Participants who heard questions worded with *smashed* gave higher speed estimates and were more likely to report glass at the scene than participants who heard *hit*. In another example, wording as simple as introducing an idea, such as asking "Did they arrive in a red car?" when the car was not red, may lead to later reports that the car was red (Scullin & Ceci, 2001). Given that older children show better memory than younger children, it is not surprising that older children are also less suggestible than younger children. Younger children are more likely to agree to events that did not happen and are at higher risk for later retellings to include misleading information that was presented in the context of questioning (see Lamb et al., 2007b, for a review).

Another technique used in questioning contexts is the pressured interview. As with misleading questions, use of this technique may not be intentional; however, there are ways to cue the informant inadvertently that perhaps what they have said was inaccurate. The simplest way to suggest doubt is by providing direct negative feedback. For example, an interviewer might say, "Other children answered this question differently, would you like to change your answer?," or "The other kids said [specific event details]." Whereas this type of pressure is not condoned in real interviews, it is used in research contexts to understand the extent to which social pressure affects children's willingness to change their responses. Another form of pressure is repeating questions, often after providing negative feedback such as "You got some of the answers wrong so I will ask you the questions again." Even without negative feedback, children may interpret a repeated question as indicating that their first answer was incorrect (Krähenbühl et al., 2009). Karpinski and Scullin (2009) found that pressured interviews led to more errors than misleading questions in three- to five-year-old children. Moreover, there is variability in the extent to which children assent to suggestive questions or pressured interviews. For example, Uhl et al. (2016) found that five- to seven-year-old children showed one of two patterns: They either gave almost all "yes" responses or almost all "no" responses to misleading questions. Uhl et al. interpreted this pattern as children either being suggestible (by saying "yes") or not (by saying "no"). However, the findings could merely reflect a response bias, with some children responding yes all the time and others responding no all the time. Unfortunately, Uhl et al. did not include control (nonleading) questions to rule out this alternative interpretation.

Younger children may be more suggestible than older children for a number of reasons. Some explanations emphasize children's cognitive immaturity, such as lacking the skills needed to meet the tasks demanded of an interview context (i.e., working memory or executive functions). Other explanations tap into the social-cognitive context, such as children may not understand that the person asking the questions does not know what happened or children's reluctance to disagree with authority figures.

A goal of anyone working with children is to provide a context where children can show their best abilities. One way to do that is to simplify the task. Asking questions that only require a yes or no response seems like a good strategy. However, this strategy may backfire because children, especially those under the age of six, have a "yes" bias (Okanda & Itakura, 2010; Okanda et al., 2013; see Fitzley et al., 2011, for a review). When asked yes/no questions, including about things they know or to questions that do not make sense, children tend to say "yes" (Hughes & Grieve, 1980). This tendency then is likely to lead children to agree to misleading questions.

Inhibiting the tendency to say "yes" may be one cognitive factor, and specifically one executive function, that influences suggestibility. As mentioned earlier, executive function is a general term describing the mental processes that allow us to plan, pay attention, and execute multiple tasks successfully (Garon et al., 2008; Muller & Kerns, 2015). Karpinski and Scullin (2009) showed that executive function predicts resistance to suggestibility particularly under pressured interview contexts. In their study, children three to five years of age with higher executive function scores were less likely to change their answers when told that some of their answers were incorrect or that other children gave different answers.

Interviews occur in a social context (even when the interviewer may be a robot! Okanda et al., 2018). Thus, a number of contextual factors are at play, many having to do with the people involved in the interaction. One unwritten assumption in such an interaction is that the person questioning the child does not know what happened. In order for children to understand that others may not know what happened, they need to have developed a theory of mind (Wellman, 2014). Theory of mind involves understanding that our minds direct our knowledge, beliefs, and desires, which in turn guide our actions. Key to this understanding is an awareness that people have different beliefs and desires, and that beliefs can be wrong (called false belief understanding; see Hughes & Devine, 2015, for a review). False belief understanding may be especially relevant to an interview context, particularly one with misleading questions.

The challenge of false belief understanding is holding two propositions in mind at the same time: your belief and the other's belief, one of which is not true. Consider the contents false belief task used by Karpinski and Scullin (2009, p. 755), which is often used to study false belief understanding in children. In this task, children see a clearly labeled Band-Aid box. Before opening the box, the experimenter says, "Here is a Band-Aid box. What do you think is inside the box?" After children say "Band-Aids," the experimenter reveals a toy pig inside the box. The box is closed and the experimenter again asks what is inside the box. Next, a toy figure is introduced as Peter, and the experimenter says "This is Peter. Peter has never seen inside the box. What does Peter think is inside the box?" Finally, the children are asked, "Did Peter see inside the box?" To pass this task and thus demonstrate false belief understanding, children must say that Peter thinks there are Band-Aids in the box and that Peter did not see inside the box. The typical error is that children say that Peter thinks there is a pig inside the box even though he did not look inside the box. Children begin to show correct responding around 4.5 years (Wellman, 2014). Returning to suggestibility, children aged three to five years who have a more advanced understanding of false beliefs are less likely to assent to misleading questions and succumb to a pressuring interviewer (Karpinski & Scullin, 2009). Presumably, these children can tell that interviewers are incorrect in their beliefs and thus do not succumb to their misleading questions or pressure to change their answers.

Another aspect of the interview context is who is doing the questioning. Children at least by six years of age are aware of the difference between retelling styles when prompted to be accurate versus entertaining (Kulkofsky et al., 2011). However, it is unclear whether children automatically notice the cues that suggest the seriousness of the situation, especially if they are not prompted to be accurate. One such cue might be signs of authority, such as the interviewer wearing a police uniform. Despite cuing that the context is serious, the presence of a uniform may lead to *less* accurate reporting. For example, four-year-old children gave inaccurate testimony when a uniformed officer suggested that something bad might have happened before they were questioned about an event compared to when the officer was not present (Tobey & Goodman, 1992). Yet, children in this study were not willing to concede to a question about potential abuse occurring, such as spanking or taking one's clothes off. Similarly, nine- to ten-year-olds erroneously selected perpetrators from lineups, especially when the actual perpetrator was absent, when asked to do so by a uniformed officer compared with a plain-clothes officer (Lowenstein et al., 2010). Lowenstein et al. (2010) suggested that the presence of the uniform cued children to believe that the police had found the perpetrator and only needed verification. Moreover, Lowenstein et al. suggested that the lack of a response (or saying "I don't know") produces anxiety over failing the identification task. As a result, children's desire to comply with an authority figure may lead them to identification errors.

Another type of question that can lead to inaccurate reporting is unanswerable questions, or a question that is not intended to be misleading (thus it is direct) but asks about something the witness never saw or experienced. In real-world contexts, these types of questions are likely to occur given that the interviewer does not know what happened, and thus may ask questions that

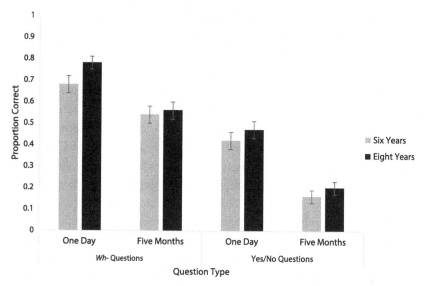

Figure 8 Mean proportion correct as a function of age, interview delay (one day or five months), and the type of question asked (*Wh-* questions or yes/no questions). All of the questions were unanswerable so a correct response is "I don't know." **Note:** Figure created by M. E. Arterberry using data from Table 1 in Waterman and Blades (2013). Error bars indicate standard error.

are unanswerable (e.g., asking, "Did she have a pen in her purse?" when the witness did not see inside the purse). Unanswerable questions can be asked in such a way that the answer is yes/no or the answer is some detail of the event (often a *Wh-* question). These types of questions are particularly difficult for children, especially when interviewed after a delay (Waterman & Blades, 2013). Even by eight years of age, children were accurate only about 33 percent of the time when asked about an event that took place five months ago (Waterman & Blades, 2013; Figure 8). Moreover, at the start of the interview, they were told that it was OK if they did not know the answer to the questions. Waterman and Blades (2013) suggested that children guess when presented with unanswerable questions; however, they found that this tendency depends on children's academic self-confidence and verbal ability. In other words, children who had higher confidence in their academic skills and higher scores on receptive vocabulary were more likely to reply "don't know" to *Wh-* questions.

5.2 Intervening Events and Source Monitoring

In addition to others asking questions in ways that might influence children's (and adults') memory for the details of events, other sources of contamination might intervene between experiencing an event and being questioned about it. One of those sources is called post-event information. For example, others around the child may discuss the event either directly with the child or amongst themselves within the child's hearing. In this context, the original memory trace is likely to be altered. This alteration can go one of two ways. One way is to the positive: Others who discuss the event may enable children to refresh their memory, or in the language of information processing, help children retrieve and re-encode (or rehearse) the details and thus strengthen recall at a later date (Roediger & Butler, 2011). In the study by Ornstein et al. (2006), asking children questions at the three-month period was designed to test the effectiveness of being questioned midway through the retention interval of six months. Recall that this three-month questioning did not strengthen children's memory. This lack of an effect may have been due to the fact that children had already forgotten key details and thus being asked questions did not help them retrieve details. It is possible that questioning before three months may have resulted in a different outcome because less information might have been lost, a possibility supported by Principe et al. (2000), who found that questions at six weeks supported retrieval at twelve weeks. Moreover, the researchers in Ornstein et al. (2006) were careful not to give the children feedback. If children did not remember a detail, they were not told what it was. In everyday interactions, parents and others might tell the child what they (the parents) thought happened or may interpret the event differently from the children. This information, whether accurate or not, may be encoded with the children's memory of the event and perhaps retrieved at a later time. Encouraging children to talk about events, particularly when using elaborative talk, improves their retention for details (Hedrick et al., 2009; Peterson et al., 2007). For example, elaborative talk during or after an event facilitated three- to six-year-olds' memory of a mock camping trip (Hedrick et al., 2009). Children who experienced elaborative talk both during and after the event showed the highest level of memory three weeks following the event. Elaborative conversations during the event likely allow children to encode the event more deeply than nonelaborative conversations. Moreover, elaborative conversations after the event allow for opportunities for retrieval practice and re-encoding, both processes that enhance retention (Roediger & Karpicke, 2006). Finally, elaborative conversations model how one talks about events, and children of highly elaborative parents provide more complete narratives when reporting on past events than children of low elaborative parents (Salmon & Reese, 2015).

Unfortunately, post-event conversations open up the potential for errors, such as misinformation. Parents and others can introduce false information, and children may include this information in later reports (Poole & Lindsay, 1995).

Keeping track of which information was provided by whom or when it was acquired (e.g., before or after the central event) is referred to as source monitoring (Johnson et al., 1993). In addition to encoding and storing details about the event itself, adults store information about the source. Children may confuse multiple sources of information about the same event, resulting in mixing details about events they experienced (a target event and a similar nontarget event) and/or heard about later. For example, Principe et al. (2000) noted which children in their study returned to their pediatric clinic after the well-child visit before the follow-up interview. In addition, they showed a subset of their original sample a video of a child receiving a well-child visit in the intervening period between their own visit and the follow-up interview. For both groups, accuracy of recall was less than those children who had no intervening events. Moreover, when mothers were asked to talk with their children about an event the children experienced at their early education program, children reported inaccurate information introduced by the mothers (as instructed by the researchers; Principe et al., 2017). Not all children reported the misinformation, however, and this difference depended on mothers' conversation styles. Children were most likely to report the misinformation when their mothers engaged in more elaborative conversation compared with less and were more controlling of the conversation and thus did not allow the children autonomy in the interaction which might enable the children to disagree with the mothers.

Another source of post-event information is repeated or similar events. For example, Ornstein et al. (2006) realized that some children may see their doctor for other reasons besides a well-child visit. Thus, the researchers took a photo of the child during their well-child checkup to cue the children which visit the interviewers were interested in when questioned later. Indeed, similar intervening events can disrupt memory. Children often experience repeated events – getting up, going to school, recess, and the like. Although many days have structure, there are deviations across repeated events (e.g., having story hour before rather than after recess, or reading a different story each day during story hour). Brubacher et al. (2011) investigated children's memory for details of six activities (e.g., counting, storybook, making a picture) that repeated four times across two weeks. They manipulated different components such that some activities were high frequency (e.g., used hand sanitizer to "refresh" three out of four times), low frequency (used a fan to "refresh" once), variable (e.g., content of the story across the four events), and new (e.g., only once did they meet a walrus). After experiencing the activities, researchers interviewed four- to five-year-olds and seven- to eight-year-olds approximately one week later. The interview began by allowing the children to report on what they remembered best. Probes were used to encourage children to provide more details (such as "tell me more"). Then, specific questions were asked about components of the activities that had not already been described. Children of both ages were best at recalling high-frequency activities, and there were no age differences. Older children recalled more low-frequency, variable, and new activities than younger children, and generally performance by the younger children for these activities was poor. Thus, components of events that repeat with high frequency are likely to be remembered better than those with low frequency or that are variable. Moreover, novel components, within the context of repeated activities, are less likely to be remembered. Confusion about details from repeated events should not be surprising given children's challenges with source monitoring and temporal ordering of activities within a single event (e.g., Arterberry & Albright, 2020; Principe et al., 2000).

One question Brubacher et al. (2011) did not ask the children was how many times the activities occurred. For example, the children engaged in four series of activities, and each time they read a storybook, three times they used hand sanitizer, but only one time they used a fan. Reporting on how many times repeated events took place is relevant to forensic contexts because it determines whether the crime was a single act or multiple viola- tions (Wandry et al., 2012). Little research has looked specifically at chil- dren's ability to recall the numerosity of events, but one study focused on six- to ten-year-olds who were removed from their homes due to suspected maltreatment. Wandry et al. (2012) asked them to report the number of foster placements and court visits after age three years. Overall, performance was poor even when given the option to respond "one or more than one" time. Similarly, Roberts et al. (2015) found that only 25 percent of four- to eight- year-old children were able to indicate how many times they engaged in repeated events after only a one-week delay. Thus, like temporal and spatial knowledge, numerical information about repeated events is difficult to access by young children.

5.3 Summary

Original memories may be corrupted in a number of ways. The way wit- nesses are questioned may not only lead to inaccurate reports due to mislead- ing questions, but the information introduced in misleading questions may be re-encoded such that subsequent retellings contain false information. Also, repeated questioning may lead witnesses to doubt what they experienced, and thus change their report. Pressure during an interview and the presence of authority figures also can result in errors, and difficulty in keeping track of sources and repeated events contribute to memory errors. These errors are not specific to children. For example, adults also face challenges in source monitoring and are susceptible to misleading questions (Mitchell et al., 2003).

6 Individual Differences

According to a forensic interviewer, some children are amazingly good in recounting event details but others are terrible (Hatch, personal communication). What is striking about this comment is that the "amazing" children are not necessarily older than the "terrible" children. A number of factors support accurate memory for events. These factors vary among children, but these factors may not necessarily be correlated with age. In other words, individual differences across children of the same age may result in greater or lesser accuracy when recounting event details.

The origins of individual differences are typically not known; however, many of the areas explored below are transmitted through interactions with other people. Thus, this section touches on several topics depicted in Figure 3 that connect to individual differences and the larger context. It is likely that the origins of these individual differences and the pathways of these developmental processes are largely social. Because of the variation in children's experiences, not all children are on the same developmental pathway at the same time, so some children will be more advanced in some areas compared with other areas and other children. Sociocultural theory helps us understand these processes. Originally proposed by Vygotsky (Miller, 2002) and expanded upon by Rogoff (2014), this perspective conceives of the child as in-activity-in-context. The context at a micro level may be the child and one other person. However, the activities and the underlying assumptions of their engagement come from the larger social context. For example, does one eat with cutlery, chop sticks, or fingers? This choice varies across cultures, and it is not decided by any one caregiver, but rather the whole community. Another feature of this perspective is the role of the more-experienced person in the dyad. These more-skilled others engage children such that children have the opportunity to function at a more advanced level than they would if alone. Whether called the zone of proximal development by Vygotsky or guided participation by Rogoff, the outcome is the opportunity to learn through activity with another person.

In this section, several culturally ascribed areas are described, with an eye toward considering how development in these domains might support accurate memory for events. Specifically, this section addresses language development, understanding right from wrong, understanding emotions, and how children acquire and organize knowledge. To greater and lesser extents, this research was conducted with children's event memory in mind. Thus, readers may be surprised by some of the topics that are included, but hopefully readers will see a case being made for how changes in these domains might support (or not) reliable memory.

6.1 Language and Nonverbal Forms of Communication

Many events involve both actions and communication, such as speech, and most interview contexts involve verbal reports. Moreover, in some contexts, witnesses may only hear what is going on, such as when a bystander cannot see an interaction but can hear the conversation (an "earwitness" context; Burrell et al., 2016). Thus, it is not surprising that limitations associated with language development have long been the number one suspect in terms of explaining why children have difficulty reporting on events. One example was noted in Section 4.1. A possible explanation for children's inability to report on the temporal ordering of events was a lack of understanding of the temporal terms *before* and *after*. Recall that children use these terms before they fully understand their meaning, but this protracted development did not explain the difficulty children had with reporting the temporal order of events (Arterberry & Albright, 2020).

A number of researchers have considered the connection between language and event memory. Some researchers, such as Ornstein et al. (2006), assessed children's vocabulary and used this information in their analyses to rule out alternative explanations based on language. For example, in Ornstein et al. (2006), all of the analyses controlled for children's performance on the Peabody Picture Vocabulary Test (PPVT), (Dunn & Dunn, 1981), a standardized measure of child language, and the researchers still found age differences in children's ability to remember the details of the well-child visit. This finding makes two points: (a) memory and forgetting were not dependent on language ability and (b) knowledge of the well-child visit was independent of vocabulary, which is often used as a proxy for general intelligence.

Instead of using measures of language as a control, other researchers focus directly on language and how it may or may not facilitate memory (e.g., Chae & Ceci, 2005; Kulkofsky, 2010). There are two measures of language to consider. The first is expressive language, or the language a child produces (also called productive language). This dimension of language may include spoken vocabulary, sentence structure, and pragmatics or the social uses of language, such as when to use "please" and "thank you," or formal versus informal verb forms in some languages (e.g., using "habla" versus "hablas" in Spanish). The second is receptive language, or the language the child understands (the PPVT measures receptive language). Klemfuss (2015) noted that studies linking language and memory have provided mixed results. One reason for these mixed findings may be the type of language assessed, namely, expressive or receptive, and the task. To tease these issues apart, Klemfuss assessed both receptive and expressive language and tested children in a memory task that involved free recall, direct questions, and misleading prompts. In this study, 2.5- to 5.5-year-old children came to the laboratory and played a game with an experimenter. They were immediately questioned about the events and then again three days later. Three weeks later, children watched a video of a birthday party, which is a standard part of the Video Suggestibility Scale for Children (Scullin & Ceci, 2001). Four days later, they were interviewed about the video. Klemfuss found that different language skills predicted performance on different types of memory tasks. Specifically, expressive language predicted children's free recall (questions that begin with "tell me what happened"). Receptive language predicted children's resistance to misleading questions. There was no difference in performance on direct questions ("What is the name of the bear in the book?").

In light of the concern over language skills limiting accurate reporting of events, some researchers proposed other ways that children might communicate what happened. One example is asking children to arrange pictures in order (e.g., Arterberry & Albright, 2020; Fivush et al., 1984; Sutherland et al., 2003). Others have attempted to use toys or props, such as anatomically correct dolls; however, use of these materials have met with mixed success in eliciting accurate information from children (Faller, 2005; Poole & Bruck, 2012). Of concern is that children might see the context as one of play in which imaginative activities are appropriate. Another concern is that interviewers need to know in advance what type of props or toys might be useful to have at the interview, but they may not know enough about the event to be prepared.

Another technique is asking children to draw a picture. Children's drawings vary widely in terms of their representational nature, accuracy, and sophistication, so the actual content of the drawing cannot replace a verbal report (Bornstein & Putnick, 2019). Instead, interviewing children while they are drawing has been found to elicit more information than a traditional verbal interview, at least under certain conditions (Barlow et al., 2011; Butler et al., 1995; Gardner et al., 2020; Gross & Hayne, 1999). Specifically, children report more event details, particularly about objects and people, when they draw and tell what the drawing is about at the same time. The amount of information is even greater when the interviewer asks questions prompting elaboration (e.g., "Can you tell me more about the bus?") versus noncommittal responses (e.g., "Oh, really?"; Barlow et al., 2011). The timing of the drawing and the interview are important: They need to co-occur such that children are drawing-while-telling. Drawing-while-telling is particularly helpful for children with poor memory abilities. Gardner et al. (2020) classified a sample of five- and six-year-old children as having poor or good working memory capacity. Children with poor working memory recounted about half of the details as children with good working memory. However, this difference disappeared when the children were asked to recount details while drawing. Both poor and good working memory groups reported the same number of details. Whether drawing-while-telling enables younger children to report more details about events than telling only is an open question because there is little research on children younger than five years of age (Bruck et al., 2000; Butler et al., 1995).

The mechanism underlying the facilitative nature of drawing has yet to be determined; however, Gardner et al. (2020) described several possibilities. First, across all studies using drawing, the interview is longer for children in the drawing condition than in the telling-only condition. It is possible that more time spent with the interviewer results in more details. However, time on task is not the whole story. Interviews are longer when children have more to say while they are drawing. Most children spontaneously talk while drawing, and it is possible that drawing facilitates retrieval in at least two ways. Images help the children report on features of the items (such as the color of the bus), and images allow children to keep track of what they have and have not reported. The drawing-while-telling context allows children to return to previous topics and add more details. Drawings serving as retrieval cues while reporting on events may also explain why the act of drawing *before* reporting (or drawing as a means of rehearsal) is not effective. When children are asked to draw after the event but before an interview, whether immediately or a few weeks later, they report more details about the event than children who do not draw, but children who draw also have higher rates of inaccuracies (Bruck et al., 2000; Otgaar et al., 2016; Teoh & Chang, 2018).

Even though the focus of the drawing-while-telling context has been on ways to help children communicate, this context also impacts the interviewer. Gardner et al. (2020) classified interviewers' responses to children's comments while children were drawing and telling. The researchers noted free-recall invitations (e.g., "Tell me everything you can remember."), direct questions that allowed for open-ended answers (e.g., "Where did you go?"), direct questions that allowed for yes/no answers, and minimal, or noncommittal, responses (e.g., "hu huh"). Interviewers were twice as likely to comment to children in a drawing-while-telling condition versus a telling-only condition. Moreover, interviewers made three times as many minimal responses to children in the drawing-while-telling condition than the verbal-only condition. Support for the bidirectional effects of drawing on children and interviewers comes from the fact that the number of interviewer comments significantly predicted the amount of information children reported. This finding aligns well with the sociocultural perspective: Children are engaging in a social activity using language and images to communicate a past experience. What is particularly appealing is that children know something the interviewers do not (at least in real-world contexts, maybe not in experiments), and interviewers' supports, as simple as saying "uh huh" or "really," facilitate children sharing the information.

6.2 Beyond Event Knowledge

As seen in Ornstein et al. (2006), Baker-Ward et al. (2015), and Sutherland et al. (2003), knowledge of what happens in certain types of events (like a visit to the doctor, dentist, or with a pirate) enhances memory for details of specific events. There may be other types of knowledge that affect how events are perceived or experienced that then also affect accurate reporting. One possibility is understanding the difference between right and wrong and the other is understanding emotions.

6.2.1 Understanding Right from Wrong

Eyewitness testimony, at least in the courts, often focuses on events that involve harm to someone or to an object. In other words, the context involves a moral transgression, or an act that is perceived to be wrong by the larger culture or society. The ability to identify that an act is wrong might affect the extent to which children attend to the details of the event or the effort they put into encoding because they may know that they might need to report on the event at a later time. It is also possible that a transgression garners more attention because the event is salient. By its very nature, it deviates from the norm.

Children as young as three years understand the basic idea of right versus wrong (Mascaro & Sperber, 2009); however, children's views on morality differ depending on various factors, such as transgression type and the relationship they have to the individuals involved. For example, Smetana and Ball (2018) found that four- to eight-year-old children viewed physical harm (e.g., shoving, see example in Section 1.1) as more wrong and more deserving of punishment compared to resource violations (e.g., sharing snacks unfairly) or psychological harm (e.g., teasing). Smetana and Ball (2018) suggested that children view physical harm as worse than other types of harm because it is more concrete and easily observed. Children in Smetana and Ball's (2018) study also viewed moral transgressions differently depending on their relationship to the individuals involved in the situation. Participants judged transgressions against bullies as most acceptable, followed by disliked peers, and then friends.

Some aspects of the eyewitness testimony context involve moral decision-making. First, children have to know that someone may have done something wrong. In addition, children need to know the implications of their testimony, such as telling the truth or selecting a perpetrator from a lineup (or not). Children are particularly poor at identifying perpetrators (e.g., Lowenstein et al., 2010). Lineups can be either simultaneous, where all the suspects appear at one time, or sequential, where the suspects appear one at a time. Lineups can also be target-present or target-absent. If police suspect the correct perpetrator, the lineup is target-present. However, if police are incorrect, the lineup is target-absent. Generally, higher accuracy of identification of perpetrators happens in simultaneous lineups compared with sequential lineups (Steblay et al., 2001). For example, when children ages seven to sixteen years were presented with simultaneous target-present lineups, they made more correct identifications (Brackmann et al., 2019), and generally children aged nine years and older make significantly more accurate identifications when presented with target-present lineups than when they were presented with target-absent lineups (Lowenstein et al., 2010). When the same event (e.g., taking a gym bag) is framed negatively (such as stealing) versus positively (helping someone), children's willingness to identify a target became more conservative with age in the stealing scenario, likely because they understood the implications of a false identification (Spring et al., 2013).

Moral evaluations of individuals based on their actions also affect memory for details of events, not just the identification of the target. Children as young as three years of age make evaluative judgments (like mean versus nice) and show a preference for nice people over mean people (Baltazar et al., 2012; Van de Vondervoort & Hamlin, 2017). In addition, children as young as four years remember the actions of mean versus nice people. Baltazar et al. (2012) showed four-year-olds pictures of people who were described as mean or nice and why (e.g., she is nice because she shares her cookies, or mean because she stole the cookies). Not only did the children remember who was mean or nice (out of eight targets), they also remembered the actions (such as who shared or stole the cookies) with an accuracy close to 80 percent. In addition, negatively described actors, such as being clumsy or messy, led to more accurate memory for event details by four- to nine-year-olds compared to when no information was provided (Cordon et al., 2016).

6.2.2 Understanding Emotions

Understanding emotions – what they are, what situations elicit them, how they guide behavior, how they are cued to others – may also be an important development that influences accurate reporting on events. Emotions (as well as beliefs and desires) guide behavior, and understanding the way that emotions guide behavior enables others to more fully understand the behavior. One difficulty in understanding emotions is that emotions are private: Only the person feeling the emotion has access to it. However, facial expressions and other body movements provide a clue to felt emotions. Thus, to understand someone else's emotions one must also perceive facial expressions.

Although discriminating different facial expressions, such happiness versus fear, appears within the first few months of life (e.g., Bornstein & Arterberry, 2003), three- to five-year-olds rarely mention emotional or physical states of characters when retelling stories, and they have difficulty interpreting emotional states of characters immediately after the expression occurs (Hayes & Casey, 1992). Moreover, emotional understanding develops slowly across the ages of three to eleven years (Pons et al., 2004). According to Pons et al. (2004), between the ages of three and six years, emotional understanding begins by recognizing and naming emotional states. Understanding progresses to knowing which contexts elicit which emotions such that children can anticipate sadness when losing something or happiness when receiving a gift. Further development leads to understanding that emotional reactions depend on desires and that different desires can lead to different reactions by different people in the same context. Similarly, children understand that beliefs, whether true or not, can lead to different emotions. Beyond six years, children begin to use strategies to regulate emotions, including hiding them. Later still, children understand that a person can have mixed emotions. Finally, children understand how positive and negative moral actions elicit different emotions.

Linking emotional understanding and face identification, Arterberry et al. (2020) found that children aged three to five years who had a better understanding of emotions were better able to identify faces with happy expressions across different viewpoints (e.g., frontal versus three-quarter profile). Children's performance with sad targets was not significantly different from chance, suggesting that facial recognition is particularly difficult for faces showing a sad facial expression. Similarly, Hayes and Casey (1992) evaluated the degree to which children could correctly label or describe specific reactions, and they reported that it was easier for three- to five-year-old children to label happiness compared with unhappiness. One reason for reduced performance with sad compared with happy faces may be because children may not see many examples of adults expressing sad emotions compared with happy emotions in their everyday contexts. Differential experience affects perception and discrimination of expressions (Pollak & Kistler, 2002; Szekely et al., 2014), and differentiation of sad expressions has a more protracted developmental timetable than happy expressions and may not reach adult levels even by thirteen years of age (Gao & Maurer, 2010).

Thus, understanding emotions may affect memory for events in that children may have trouble fully understanding the events, including why they occurred, or identifying those involved. Emotional understanding also may affect attentional processes: As emotional understanding increases, children may be better able to focus on salient features of the event due to an understanding of the possible motivations behind others' actions. Additionally, the protracted development in understanding emotions may have implications for how children understand their own felt emotions and the situations that cause them. How one reacts to emotionally charged contexts has implications for one's willingness to talk about an event. For example, in a study by Walter and LaFreniere (2007), children were left in a room with an attractive toy that accidentally breaks (it was rigged to create this mishap). Children who showed a shame response were less likely to talk about the toy or to look at it once the experimenter returned. By contrast, children who showed tension or worry (operationalized as a guilt response) were more likely to confess that the toy broke and expressed a desire to help repair it. Even twenty years later, emotional impact of an event predicted adults' willingness to talk about childhood events (Goodman et al., 2019). Adults with depression or post-traumatic stress disorder (PTSD) recalled more details of childhood events than adults who did not have depression or PTSD.

6.3 Acquiring and Organizing Knowledge

The last source of individual differences to be considered in this Element is how children acquire and organize knowledge. Two developmental processes are considered: collaborative activities and semantic development. One of these processes may lead children to make memory errors, whereas the other may be protective. First consider collaborative contexts. As mentioned earlier, the sociocultural perspective emphasizes that children can learn via working with or alongside more-skilled others. One example is a study conducted by Ratner et al. (2002) in which five-year-old children engaged with an adult in a task that involved placing objects into a doll house. The children worked with the adult to plan which furniture items went in which rooms. In the collaboration condition, the children and the adult took turns placing the objects. In the no collaboration condition, the adult placed all of the objects. Next, all of the objects were removed from the doll house and the experimenter asked the children to identify who placed which object in the doll house. Finally, children were asked to categorize the objects by room type. Ratner et al. (2002) found that children in the collaboration condition made a number of errors when asked who placed which objects, attributing more placements to themselves than to the adult. At the same time, the children in the collaboration condition showed higher categorization performance than children in the no collaboration condition. These findings suggest that, during the interaction, children appropriated the actions of their interaction partner (a mistake) but that led to increased learning. How children collaborate and the extent to which they appropriate others' actions as their own may have implications for their accuracy in reporting on events, particularly if children were participants in the events. In other words, children may be more likely to claim they did something when they did not. Thus, a developmental process that in many ways promotes positive cognitive outcomes may inadvertently lead to inaccurate reporting of events.

A second developmental process may serve as a protective factor regarding testimony errors. Semantic development pertains to the acquisition of knowledge. Adults not only have pieces of knowledge, but the pieces are organized in such a way that they can make connections among ideas and concepts. When encountering new information and experiences, it is often linked it to what is already known. This linking then facilitates retrieval. One way to gain insight into this process is the Deese/Roediger-McDermott (DRM) paradigm (Deese, 1959; Roediger & McDermott, 1995). In the DRM paradigm, participants hear a list of words aligned with a theme, such as food, dough, crust, and toast related to the word *bread*. The critical lure, *bread*, is associated with all of the words in the list, but it is never presented. At test, adults incorrectly recognize the critical lure about 80 percent of the time (Anastasi & Rhodes, 2008; Brainerd et al., 2002). This reporting of a word that was never presented is called a false memory. Across numerous studies, children report the crucial lure less than adults. For example, Anastasi and Rhodes (2008) found that children, aged five through eight years, recognized the critical lure 57 percent of the time, and Brainerd et al. found that children aged five years and eleven years recognized the critical lure 65 and 56 percent of the time, respectively. Similarly, Howe et al. (2010) found a developmental trend among children, where seven-year-olds falsely recalled (23 percent) and recognized (58 percent) significantly fewer critical lures than eleven-year-olds (33 and 70 percent for recall and recognition, respectively). Likelihood to recall the critical lure continues to increase between twelve and twenty-one years of age (McGuire et al., 2015).

Researchers propose two explanations for false memory. The first is that children are unable to extract the gist or central theme of the list (such as fifteen words related to *bread*), and thus they do not recall or recognize the word *bread* (e.g., Brainerd et al., 2002). A second explanation appeals to the organization of concepts in semantic memory such that greater organization will lead to spreading activation (Roediger & McDermott, 1995). The idea is that when hearing the words food, dough, crust, and the like, the words are located close to each other and close to bread. Thus, bread becomes activated, and later retrieved, even though the word was not presented. Evidence supporting both of these explanations comes from the fact that reporting of the critical lure is reduced when lists do not contain strong associations among the list items and the critical lure (e.g., Brainerd et al., 2002) and that embedding the list items in a story that was biased away from the critical lure (such as the critical lure of *lion* in a story about a costume party versus a circus) decreased children's reporting of the critical lure (Howe & Wilkinson, 2011). Teasing apart these two explanations is beyond the scope of this Element; however, both point to the same conclusion. Children report fewer false memories because of their immature semantic development.

6.4 Summary

Language development plays an important role in eyewitness testimony, and it intersects in various ways such that some tasks (e.g., resistance to misleading questions) rely on receptive language, whereas other tasks (e.g., free recall) rely on expressive language. There are ways that interviewers can compensate for children's language skills, such as using hierarchical questioning (asking children to first recall all that they remember and then using direct questions to probe for more information) and drawing-while-telling. Understanding right from wrong, and the development of this understanding, has implications for memory accuracy. What is considered right versus wrong varies by culture, and these conventions are likely transmitted to children in different ways by others in the children's environment. Emotions, how they are felt, interpreted, and displayed are also culturally specified, and children's understanding of emotion may affect face recognition and other aspects of events. Other cognitive developments have implications for accurate reporting of events, such that collaborative learning contexts may increase memory errors, whereas underdeveloped semantic memory may serve as a protective factor for an age group that has other challenges in accurately reporting on events.

7 Adults' Perceptions of Child Eyewitnesses

Understanding what factors influence children's accuracy in reporting on events has important practical implications. Children's reports of crimes, either experienced directly or witnessed as a bystander, play a role in prosecution and securing children's safety. Moreover, in cases of abuse, children may be the only witness to a crime. Thus, the success of any court proceeding depends on how others, especially potential jurors, perceive the reliability of children's reports of events. Consequently, a number of researchers have investigated this question.

Among the first researchers to ask the question about children's reliability were Goodman et al. (1987). In their first two experiments, they presented college-aged students written descriptions of vehicle–pedestrian accident or a murder. In both studies, the key eyewitness, a bystander, was six, ten, or thirty years of age. Participants rated the degree of guilt of the defendant and credibility of the eyewitness. Across both crimes, witness credibility increased with age but degree of defendant guilt did not. A third study used videotaped testimony of a vehicle–pedestrian accident and a community sample of potential jurors. Again, credibility ratings increased with age of the witness, whereas degree of the defendant's guilt did not. Since this early work, a number of studies have looked at a variety of crimes (abuse, robbery, vehicle accidents), ages of children, extralegal features of potential jurors (e.g., age or gender), and method of testimony. This section begins by describing one ambitious study conducted by Wright et al. (2010) to set the stage for this type of research and to highlight some methodological considerations. After presentation of the results, the findings of Wright et al. (2010) are compared with those found by other researchers.

7.1 Child Witness and Potential Juror Factors

To understand the extent to which child factors, such as age and sex, participant factors, such as age and gender, and type of event (sexual or physical abuse) impact perceptions of child eyewitnesses, Wright et al. (2010) tested adults' perceptions of child eyewitnesses at eleven different ages: three, four, five, six, seven, eight, nine, ten, twelve, fifteen, and eighteen years. A community sample of adults (mean age was thirty-three years) read an approximately 280-word vignette in which a boy or girl bystander witnessed either physical or sexual abuse. The alleged physical abuse was between the witness's parents and took place in the home, and the alleged sexual abuse was between a teacher and a student and took place in a school. This design resulted in forty-four different vignettes by crossing age of child, sex of child, and type of crime. Adult participants were approached in public places in Southwest England and asked to participate in this short study. They read one of the vignettes and then provided a verdict: defendant was guilty or not guilty. Next, participants rated their beliefs in guilt of the defendant on a scale of 0–100, the child witness's memory reliability on a scale of 0–10, and the child witness's honesty on a scale of 0–10 (in all three ratings higher values indicated higher belief, reliability, and honesty). Finally, participants provided their age and gender. (Following Wright et al., 2010, for sex, boy and girl are used to describe the children, and for gender, male and female are used to describe the adult respondents.)

7.1.1 A Methodological Aside

Consider some of the decisions Wright et al. (2010) made in the design of this study. First, they tested a community sample. Much psychological research is conducted with college or university students because it is convenient (they often participate for course credit). It is true that in most countries people over the age of eighteen are potential jurors; however, in practice, the average age of juries is well beyond eighteen to twenty-two (which is the traditional age of students in college/university in the United States.). One estimate of average juror age is forty-three years, well beyond the age of most college/university students (Anwar et al., 2014). A community sample – in this case shoppers in the marketplace – varies in age and experience, and they are more representative of the typical jury pool than college/university students. A second decision was including many ages for the child witness. Typically, researchers compare several age groups, such as two children with a young adult, as seen in Goodman et al. (1987). Testing only a few ages reduces the overall number of conditions (Goodman et al. had three conditions) and the number of participants who need to be tested (Goodman et al. tested an average of seventy-four per experiment). In contrast, Wright et al. (2010) had forty-four conditions as a result of eleven witness ages, two witness sexes, and two events. Using more ages allowed for the identification of developmental trends, particularly those that may not be linear (Bainter et al., 2020), but it also means a much larger sample size (the final sample was 607 participants in Wright et al., 2010). A third consideration made by Wright et al. (2010) was including both boy and girl eyewitnesses. Many studies, especially those focusing on sexual abuse scenarios, feature only girl witnesses (e.g., Antrobus et al., 2016; Brigham, 1998). The inclusion of boys as witnesses provides a full picture of how witnesses of both sexes are perceived by potential jurors.

Wright et al. (2010) also made the decision to use a short vignette. Across studies, there is considerable variability in materials used, from video or audio recordings of real or mock testimony, verbatim transcripts, and short or long summaries. For example, McCauley and Parker (2001) used a nine-page transcript, and Antrobus et al. (2016) provided different forms of video (in court, prerecorded at the time of the first complaint, and CCTV video link the day before a trial). A short summary reduces the time it takes to complete the study, a concern that is especially relevant if one is testing participants in public venues as opposed to research laboratories or classrooms. The support of Wright et al.'s decision to use short vignettes is evidence that mode of presentation of the testimony, specifically written versus video, does not change the pattern of results (e.g., Bornstein, 1999; Goodman et al., 1987).

7.1.2 Now for Some Results

For memory reliability and honesty, Wright et al. (2010) found nonlinear trends in adults' perceptions. Overall, children's perceived memory reliability significantly increased between ages three and six and then remained relatively stable until eighteen years of age (Figure 9). However, perception of memory reliability was different for male and female respondents, such that males reported memory continuing to increase after six years, whereas females perceived no change (Figure 9). Children's perceived honesty also increased between three and six years, and then it dipped for boys from age six to fifteen and then increased again up to age eighteen (Figure 10). Girls' honesty ratings continued to increase from age six and then dropped after age twelve. By eighteen years of age, honesty ratings for both boys and girls were at the same level.

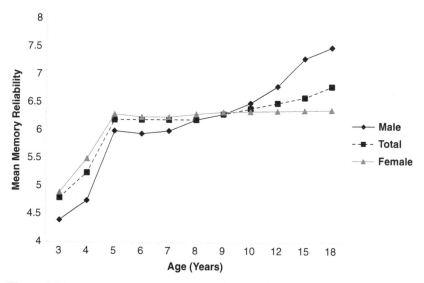

Figure 9 Memory reliability as a function of child witness age. Solid lines show ratings as a function of participant gender. Dashed line (labeled Total) shows memory reliability ratings collapsed across male and female participants.
Note: Figure reproduced by combining two graphs in Figure 2 in Wright et al. (2010) with permission by M. E. Arterberry. See original for standard error.

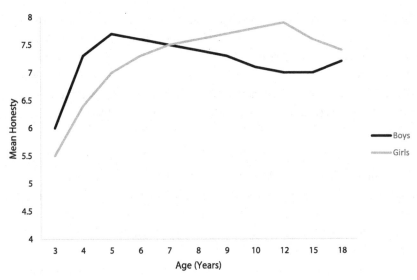

Figure 10 Perceived honesty as a function of child witness age and gender.
Note: Figure reproduced from Wright et al. (2010) with permission by M. E. Arterberry. See original for standard error.

Belief in guilt of the defendant was most affected by memory reliability ratings. High ratings for memory reliability predicted high levels of belief in guilt. Moreover, ratings of honesty had no predictive power in belief in guilt over and above memory reliability. The same pattern of results was found for the final decision of guilty or not in that memory reliability rating was a significant predictor but honesty was not. Also type of event mattered: Adults gave more guilty verdicts for the sexual abuse vignette compared with the physical abuse vignette. Finally, older participants and females gave fewer guilty verdicts.

7.1.3 Comparisons to Other Research

The finding that perceptions of children's memory reliability increased with age is consistent with other research on potential jurors. Younger children are perceived as less accurate than older children and often older children are rated as less accurate than young adults (e.g., Brigham, 1998; Bruer & Pozzulo, 2014; Nikonova & Ogloff, 2005; Nunez et al., 2011), but there are exceptions (e.g., Holcomb & Jacquin, 2007). Moreover, the nonlinear trend shown in Figure 9 was replicated by Nunez et al. (2011) using university students as respondents to vignettes where the witness was a victim in a sexual abuse scenario. Adults' perceptions of young children's memory reliability articulate with the research on children's event memory (as reviewed earlier in this Element). Children three to six years of age have challenges in remembering event details, even when asked immediately after an event, and there are few if any reported differences between boys and girls in the literature. Yet, children beyond six years of age continue to face challenges, such as temporal memory, spatial memory, suggestibility, and long delay. Thus, adults may be overly optimistic in their perceptions of the memory reliability of children aged six to twelve years of age. Accurate perception of children's memory reliability is important, given that perception of memory reliability appears to more strongly affect belief in defendant guild and guilt verdict than honesty (but see Voogt et al., 2020).

Ratings of honesty of child witnesses are not as clear as those for memory reliability. Not all researchers ask participants to rate child witness honesty (or trustworthiness or truthfulness), and some researchers find reverse trends with younger children being perceived as more honest than older children (e.g., Nikonova & Ogloff, 2005). This reverse trend may be due to the fact that in some cases, like sexual abuse, there is a belief that younger children could not be lying about details about which their age group would not normally know (Holcomb & Jacquin, 2007; Nunez et al., 2011, but see Bornstein et al., 2007). The discrepancy in findings could be due to the way honesty ratings may be affected by child witness sex and the fact that ratings appear to be nonlinear (also replicated by Nunez et al., 2011). The adults in Wright et al. (2010) may have been overly pessimistic about the honesty of children, especially because the eyewitnesses were bystanders and had little to gain or lose by telling the truth. At the same time, the adults in Wright et al. (2010) were generally accurate regarding sex differences: Boys were perceived as less honest than girls between age six and fifteen. In the early years, girls lie less than boys (Gervais et al., 2000; Watanabe & Lee, 2016). However, not all studies on lying test for child sex differences and not all find sex differences when they test for them. For example, Talwar et al. (2007) found no differences between six- to eleven-year-old boys and girls in rates of lying in a laboratory task. As children age, they become more aware of the social contexts for lying, particularly lies that are told to avoid hurting others' feelings (Harris & Gross, 1988; Talwar et al., 2019).

The participants in Wright et al. (2010) made judgments about two abuse scenarios: one physical and one sexual, in which the witness was a bystander. Most of the ratings were the same for the two types of abuse, with the exception of guilt verdict. Participants gave more guilty verdicts in the sexual abuse scenario compared to the physical abuse scenario. This finding was replicated when the witness was a victim as opposed to a bystander (Sheahan et al., 2021). Moreover, compared to other types of crimes, such as a robbery, sexual abuse scenarios result in higher conviction rates (McCauley &Parker, 2001). Abuse scenarios also illuminate gender differences among adult respondents. Females generally are more likely to render a guilty verdict than males, which may stem from greater empathy for victims of physical or sexual assault (Bottoms et al., 2014; Jones et al., 2020; Voogt et al., 2019).

Wright et al. (2010) revealed two participant factors that impact perceptions of child eyewitnesses: age and gender, which are consistent with other research (e.g., Voogt & Klettke, 2017). There may be other factors as well. Adults' past experiences with the type of crime may also impact their perceptions of child eyewitnesses (Bottoms et al., 2014; Jones et al., 2020). For example, being sexually abused or knowing someone who has been sexually abused is associated with increased victim empathy, such that adults with sexual abuse experience not only have higher levels of victim empathy but also perceive child eyewitnesses as more credible and rate defendants as guiltier than those without sexual abuse history (Jones et al., 2020). Also, experience with the legal system impacts perceptions of child eyewitnesses. Professionals who work with children in the legal system also perceive children's memory credibility and suggestibility differently from those who do not. For example, Melinder et al. (2004) found that defense attorneys were skeptical of the credibility and honesty of child eyewitnesses. Moreover, parents, educators, and experienced forensic interviewers were better at identifying children who are lying versus telling the truth than other participants who had less experience with children (Crossman & Lewis, 2006; Nysse-Carris et al., 2011; Talwar et al., 2011).

The focus of Wright et al. (2010) was on adults' perception of children's memory reliability and honesty and how these perceptions affected belief in guilt and guilt verdict. There are, however, other factors that may play a role in determining guilt. Voogt et al. (2017) list five domains: accuracy, believability, competency, reliability, and truthfulness. Video, audio, or longer written transcripts with dialog may provide additional context with which to rate these five dimensions. For example, some researchers provide enough context to determine whether children made errors in their testimony (e.g., Bruer & Pozzulo, 2014). Moreover, video enables researchers to ask questions about child confidence, likely gleaned from verbal and nonverbal cues such as powerless speech or gaze aversion, which in turn may factor into ratings of believability and competency (e.g., Antrobus et al., 2012, 2016).

7.2 Summary

Just as a number of factors influence children's ability to report accurately on events, a number of factors influence adults' perception of child eyewitnesses, including child age, child sex, participant gender, participant sex, event type, and other extralegal experiences of potential jurors. Generally, potential jurors in Wright et al. (2010) may be overly optimistic about children's ability to report on events accurately and overly pessimistic in their perceptions of children's honesty. Given the role that child witnesses play in criminal proceedings, especially in contexts such as abuse where they may be the only witness, further understanding of the factors that influence jurors' perceptions is important. As more research is conducted, the story may become increasingly complex, such that it may not be useful to talk generally about adults' perceptions (Brigham, 1998). The perceptions depend on *which* adults considering *which* children under *which* circumstances.

8 Applications

Often researchers ask and answer questions because of theoretical interest: They want to know why and how a phenomenon develops and they care less so about how their discoveries may be used. Others may see the findings and apply them. Some of the research on children's event memory started with a basic research question and led to interesting applications. Conversely, some researchers ask and answer questions because they want to solve real-world problems. Eyewitness testimony is one of those problems. By trying to determine the parameters of what children can and cannot report and the contexts that affect their reporting, researchers have revealed a number of secrets about the development of event memory. As witnessed in this Element, this two-pronged approach yielded a tremendous amount of knowledge about children's event memory, and this knowledge shapes how professionals work with children in criminal contexts today.

One result from this decades-long research agenda is best practices when children engage with the legal system. Many states in the United States, and many countries, have regulations about how and where to interview children and the type of information that is useful in a legal context. For example, some states acknowledge that children as young as three or four years may be able to testify (e.g., Maine), whereas other states indicate an age limit under which special considerations need to be made (e.g., Pennsylvania and California). Considerations regarding child testimony include both children's competency and minimizing harm.

The National Institute of Child Health and Human Development (NICHD) Revised Investigative Interview Protocol has scripted questions with guidance on how and when to interview children in order to maximize the information obtained from the children without causing additional distress or harm. Table 1 shows examples from each section of the interview. As is clear, all the prompts

Table 1 Sample questions from the National Institute of Child Health and Human Development (NICHD) Revised Investigative Interview Protocol

Section	Sample Question or Statement to Child	Guidance
Introduction	My name is ____ and my job is to talk to children about things that happen to them. As you can see, we have a video-camera here . . . . Are you comfortable?	*Gestures of goodwill are appropriate, such as "are you comfortable?"*
Rapport Building and Narrative Training	. . . I want to get to know you better. Tell me about things you like to do.	*If child responds, express appreciation and reinforcement:* Thank you for sharing . . . .
Explaining and Practicing Ground Rules	If I ask a question that you don't understand, just say, "[Interviewer's name], I don't understand." If I don't understand what you say, I'll ask you to explain. *Pause* If I ask a question, and you don't know the answer, just tell me, "I don't know." So, [child's name], if I ask you, [e.g., what did I have for breakfast today], what would you say?	*If child says "I don't know," say:* "Right. You don't know . . ."
Further Rapport Building and	A few [days, weeks] ago was [a holiday, birthday party, other event]. Tell me everything that happened	

Episodic Memory Training	[during the event], from the beginning to the end, as best as you can.	*If do not know an event in advance, ask about whether the child did something special recently or their day from the time they woke up.*
Substantive Phase	Now that we know each other a little better, I want to talk about why [you are, I am] here today. I understand something may have happened to you. Tell me everything that happened from beginning to end.	*If child reports an irrelevant event, say: " . . . we can talk about that later."*
Disclosure Information	Now I want to understand how other people found out about [last incident]. Or Does anybody know what happened?	*Then explore the disclosure process, such as time, circumstances, recipients, reactions, etc.*
Ending the Interview	What are you going to do after we finish talking?	*Talk to the child for a couple of minutes about a neutral topic.*

Source: https://nichdprotocol.com/

are open-ended such that children provide the narrative and interviewers prompt for more details using open-ended questions, such as "Can you tell me more about that?" There are no direct questions that require a specific response (e.g., "What color was the hat?"). Even though direct questions result in more accurate recall of details in laboratory contexts, they are the very questions that can lead to suggestibility and misinformation (Karpinski & Scullin, 2009). The NICHD protocol elicits high-quality information compared to other protocols (Brown et al., 2013; Lamb et al., 2007a). The protocol also prompts children to describe a wide variety of emotions that enrich the quality of the testimony, and it protects children from later misinformation (Karni-Visel et al., 2019; Otgaar et al., 2021).

In the United States, Child Advocacy Centers combine the best practices of the NICHD interview protocol with the research on factors that contaminate memories. These centers bring all parties who need to hear the testimony together such that children only have to tell their story once. In this model, the interviewer talks with the child (which is videotaped), and social workers, police officers, medical professionals, and other legal professionals observe the interaction (often from another location, such as through a two-way mirror or via a video feed). The interview takes place in a child-friendly place (not a police station), and the child is brought to the location by a trusted adult. To paraphrase the National Child Alliance, Child Advocacy Centers eliminate the need for children to tell the worst story of their lives over and over again. From a cognitive development perspective, talking about the event once eliminates the potential problem of repeated questioning and/or the potential for intervening events to occur between interviews, both of which may contaminate memory for event details.

9 Conclusion

As acknowledged at the beginning of this Element, the answer to the question about what age children can be reliable eyewitnesses is elusive. The answer may be elusive because there are many factors that influence children's accuracy in reporting on events. Moreover, a number of factors influence the extent to which others believe child eyewitnesses. Nevertheless, are there general conclusions that can be made about children's ability to report accurately about events? At risk of overgeneralizing, here are eight general conclusions about children's event memory based on the research presented in this Element. First (stating the obvious), younger children typically remember less than older children. Second, children who have knowledge or preparation about an event before it occurs are likely to remember more than children who lack the knowledge or who are not prepared. Third, children who engage in elaborative conversations with an adult (one who uses *Wh-*questions to elicit responses), either during or after the event, are likely to remember more than children who do not. Fourth, children who are securely attached to their parents are likely to remember more than children who are insecurely attached, possibly due to the fact that sensitive parenting (which forms the basis of attachment) may lead to activities like elaboration and preparation. Fifth, children are likely to remember activities engaged in more so than where the activities occurred or the temporal order of event components. Sixth, children's reporting of events is fragile, such that poorly worded questions may mislead them. Thus, the best way to elicit information is through open-ended questions ("tell me what happened") versus yes/no questions. Seventh, children may confuse different instances of repeated or similar events, and they may have trouble indicating how many times a repeated event occurred. Finally, children's reporting on events is likely supported by other developments, particularly in the areas of language, social cognition, and executive function.

Despite the large amount of knowledge gained from studies on children's eyewitness testimony, there is more work to be done. The research in this Element focused on younger children, generally aged three to eight years of age, which reflected a bias in the field for understanding the development of event memory in the youngest ages. This bias stems from the real-world question about whether young children can be reliable eyewitnesses in legal contexts. However, memory, language, and a host of other social and cognitive developments continue well into adolescence (Białecka-Pikul et al., 2020; Krettenauer et al., 2014; Meinhardt-Injac et al., 2020). Thus, a comprehensive view of what factors influence children's accuracy in reporting on events needs to include older children as well; however, there is little research that directly addresses this topic in adolescence. Given that adults perceive differences in memory reliability and honesty of children older than age eight (e.g., Wright et al., 2010), a complete understanding of the development of event memory across childhood will help those who interview children of all ages to minimize harm during questioning, and it will help adults, such as potential jurors and others in legal professions, to reliably evaluate child eyewitnesses' capabilities.

Much of the research presented in this Element focused on unique events, such as a trip to a zoo or museum, a mock camping trip, a trip to an emergency department, a visit to a research lab, unusual events in an early education program, and the like. These events are salient in that they are unique. Criminal events, such as abuse, often are repeated, and can take place over long periods of time. Thus, more research is needed with repeated, and perhaps less unique events, in order to understand the factors that affect children's memory under repeated circumstances.

Another area for future research is exploring differences across cultures. Almost all of the studies reported in this Element focused on Caucasian children and families living in English-speaking countries. Moreover, 80 percent of studies on adults' perceptions of child eyewitnesses were done in the United States and Canada (Voogt et al., 2019). Different cultures have different socialization practices and values that may impact how events are interpreted, discussed, and reminisced. For example, in a study with Norwegian children, Fonn et al. (2022) showed that three- to six-year-old children did not endorse statements from dominant others, a finding they attributed to the highly egalitarian society in Norway. This finding has implications for children's suggestibility and the potential influence of memory contamination of post-event conversations. In addition, eyewitness testimony takes place in a sociocultural context. Understanding when a wrong has been committed and understanding others' motivations, beliefs, and desires may differ across contexts with different socialization practices, and in turn may affect children's event memory.

This Element emphasized the researchers' interpretations of their findings more so than providing a critique of their work or whether their interpretations are unquestionably supported by their data. All studies have limitations, which leave findings open to alternative explanations. Thus, the conclusions herein are tentative until more research confirms these findings, such as through replication. As is typical with areas in which a large number of researchers explore a topic from different vantage points, there is variability across studies, such as type of events, assessments, and child involvement. This variability presents challenges to comparing findings across studies. Do results differ because different studies used a pediatric exam, a visit with a pirate, and a mock camping trip? Do results differ because different age groups were tested, different delays between the event and interview were used, or children were questioned in different ways? A similar challenge exists in the literature on adults' perceptions of child eyewitnesses. Different researchers measured memory, honesty, credibility, and the like in different ways; different researchers presented events as written summaries, written verbatim transcripts, or audio/video recordings of a mock court proceedings. Moving forward, it might help to compare findings across studies if researchers adopt an approach that involves replication and extension. The replication component will allow for direct comparisons to previous findings, and the extension, or novel question, will allow further understanding of the phenomena.

Everyday interactions are enriched by recounting events, and this fact is true for children. Moreover, the need for children to report on criminal events, whether they are directly involved in the event as in the case of abuse or as a bystander, is an unfortunate reality. Continued research on the development of event memory will enable better understanding of what children remember, the best timing for interviews, and the best ways to support children before, during, and after retelling contexts.

References

Ainsworth, M. D. S., & Wittig, B. A. (1969). Attachment and exploratory behavior of one-year-olds in a strange situation. In B. M. Foss (Ed.), *Determinants of infant behavior* (Vol. 4, pp. 111–136). Routledge Methuen.

Alexander, K. W., O'Hara, K. D., Bortfeld, H. V. et al. (2010). Memory for emotional experiences in the context of attachment and social interaction style. *Cognitive Development, 25*, 325–338. https://doi.org/10.1016/j.cogdev.2010.08.002

Alexander, K. W., Quas, J. A., & Goodman, G. S. (2002). Theoretical advances in understanding children's memory for distressing events: The role of attachment. *Developmental Review, 22*, 490–519. https://doi.org/10.1016/S0273-2297(02)00004-7

Anastasi, J. S., & Rhodes, M. G. (2008). Examining differences in levels of false memories in children and adults using child-normed lists. *Developmental Psychology, 44*(3), 889–894. https://doi.org/10.1037/0012-1649.44.3.889

Antrobus, E., McKimmie, B. M., & Newcombe, P. A. (2012). Community members' beliefs about children in Australian courts. *Psychiatry, Psychology and Law, 19*, 497–516. https://doi.org/10.1080/10494820.2011.615721

Antrobus, E., McKimmie, B. M., & Newcombe, P. A. (2016). Mode of children's testimony and the effect of assumptions about credibility. *Psychiatry, Psychology and Law, 23*, 922–940. https://doi.org/10.1080/13218719.2016.1152927

Anwar, S., Bayer, P., & Hjalmarsson, R. (2014). The role of age in jury selection and trial outcomes. *The Journal of Law and Economics, 57*, 1001–1030. https://doi.org/10.1086/675257

Arterberry, M. E., & Albright, E. J. (2020). Children's memory for temporal information: The roles of temporal language and executive function. *Journal of Genetic Psychology: Research and Theory on Human Development, 181*, 191–205. https://doi.org/10.1080/00221325.2020.1741503

Arterberry, M. E., Perry, E. T., Price, C. M., & Steimel, S. (2020). Emotional understanding predicts facial recognition in 3- to 5-year-old children. *European Journal of Developmental Psychology, 17*, 293–306. https://doi.org/10.1080/17405629.2019.1589445

Atkinson, R. C., & Shiffrin, R. M. (1968). Human memory: A control system and its control processes. *The Psychology of Learning and Motivation, 2*, 89–195. https://doi.org/10.1016/S0079-7421(08)60422-3

Bainter, S. A., Tibbe, T. D., Goodman, Z. T., & Poole, D. A. (2020). Child eyewitness researchers often bin age: Prevalence of the practice and recommendations for analyzing developmental trends. *Law and Human Behavior*, *44*, 327–335. https://doi.org/10.1037/lhb0000416

Baker-Ward, L., Gordon, B. N., Ornstein, P. A., Larus, D. M., & Clubb, P. A. (1993). Young children's long-term retention of a pediatric examination. *Child Development*, *64*, 1519–1533. https://doi.org/10.2307/1131550

Baker-Ward, L., Quinonez, R., Milano, M. et al. (2015). Predicting children's recall of a dental procedure: Contributions of stress, preparation, and dental history. *Applied Cognitive Psychology*, *29*, 775–781. https://doi.org/10.1002/acp.3152

Baltazar, N. C., Shutts, K., & Kinzler, K. D. (2012). Children show heightened memory for threatening social actions. *Journal of Experimental Child Psychology*, *112*, 102–110. https://doi.org/10.1016/j.jecp.2011.11.003

Barlow, C. M., Jolley, R. P., & Hallam, J. L. (2011). Drawings as memory aids: Optimizing the drawing method to facilitate young children's recall. *Applied Cognitive Psychology*, *25*, 480–487. https://doi.org/10.1002/acp.1716

Bauer, P. J., Doydum, A. O., Pathman, T. et al. (2012). It's all about location, location, location: Children's memory for the "where" of personally experienced events. *Journal of Experimental Child Psychology*, *113*, 510–522. https://doi.org/10.1016/j.jecp.2012.06.007

Bauer, P. J., Stewart, R., White, E. A., & Larkina, M. (2016). A place for every event and every event in its place: Memory for locations and activities by 4-year-old children. *Journal of Cognition and Development*, *17*, 244–263. https://doi.org/10.1080/15248372.2014.959521

Benear, S. L., Ngo, C. T., Olson, I. R., & Newcombe, N. S. (2021). Understanding relational binding in early childhood: Interacting effects of overlap and delay. *Journal of Experimental Child Psychology*, *208*, 150152. https://doi.org/10.1016/j.jecp.2021.105152

Białecka-Pikul, M., Szpak, M., Zubek, J., Bosacki, S., & Kołodziejczyk, A. (2020). The psychological self and advanced theory of mind in adolescence. *Self and Identity*, *19*, 85–104. https://doi.org/10.1080/15298868.2018.1538900

Bornstein, B. H. (1999). The ecological validity of jury simulations: Is the jury still out? *Law and Human Behavior*, *23*, 75–92. https://doi.org/10.1023/A:1022326807441

Bornstein, B. H., Kaplan, D. L., & Perry, A. R. (2007). Child abuse in the eyes of the beholder: Lay perceptions of child sexual and physical abuse. *Child Abuse & Neglect*, *31*, 375–391. https://doi.org/10.1016/j.chiabu.2006.09.007

Bornstein, M. H., & Arterberry, M. E. (2003). Recognition, categorization, and apperception of the facial expression of smiling by 5-month-old infants.

Developmental Science, 6, 585–599. https://doi.org/10.1111/1467-7687 .00314

Bornstein, M. H., & Putnick, D. L. (2019). *The architecture of the child mind: G, Fs, and the hierarchical model of intelligence.* Taylor & Francis.

Bottoms, B. L., Peter-Hagene, L. C., Stevenson, M. C. et al. (2014). Explaining gender differences in jurors' reactions to child sexual assault cases. *Behavioral Sciences & the Law, 32*(6), 789–812. https://doi.org/10.1002/bsl.2147

Bowlby, J. (1958). The nature of the child's tie to his mother. *International Journal of Psychoanalysis, 39,* 350–373.

Bowlby, J. (1969). *Attachment and loss: Attachment* (2nd ed., Vol. 1). Basic Books.

Brackmann, N., Sauerland, M., & Otgaar, H. (2019). Developmental trends in lineup performance: Adolescents are more prone to innocent bystander misidentifications than children and adults. *Memory & Cognition, 47*(3), 428–440. https://doi.org/10.3758/s13421-018-0877-6

Brainerd, C. J., Aydin, C., & Reyna, V. F. (2012). Development of dual-retrieval processes in recall: Learning, forgetting, and reminiscence. *Journal of Memory and Language, 66,* 763–788. https://doi.org/10.1016/j.jml.2011.12.002

Brainerd, C. J., Holliday, R. E., Reyna, V. F., Yang, Y., & Toglia, M. P. (2010). Developmental reversals in false memory: Effects of emotional valence and arousal. *Journal of Experimental Child Psychology, 107,* 137–154. https://doi.org/10.1016/j.jecp.2010.04.013

Brainerd, C. J., & Reyna, V. F. (1995). Learning rate, learning opportunities, and the development of forgetting. *Developmental Psychology, 31,* 251–262. https://doi.org/10.1037/0012-1649.31.2.251

Brainerd, C. J., Reyna, V. F., & Forrest, T. J. (2002). Are young children susceptible to the false-memory illusion? *Child Development, 73*(5), 1363–1377. https://doi.org/10.1111/1467-8624.00477

Brigham, J. C. (1998). Adults' evaluations of characteristics of children's memory. *Journal of Applied Developmental Psychology, 19,* 15–39. https://doi.org/10.1016/S0193-3973(99)80026-4

Brown, D. A., Lamb, M. E., Lewis, C. et al. (2013). The NICHD Investigative Interview Protocol: An analogue study. *Journal of Experimental Psychology: Applied, 19,* 367–382. https://doi.org/10.1037/a0035143

Brubacher, S. P., Glisic, U., Roberts, K. P., & Powell, M. (2011). Children's ability to recall unique aspects of one occurrence of a repeated event. *Applied Cognitive Psychology, 25,* 351–358. https://doi.org/10.1002/acp.1696

Bruck, M., Melnyk, L., & Ceci, S. J. (2000). Draw it again Sam: The effect of drawing on children's suggestibility and source monitoring ability. *Journal of*

Experimental Child Psychology, *77*, 169–196. https://doi.org/10.1006/jecp.1999.2560

Bruer, K., & Pozzulo, J. D. (2014). Influence of eyewitness age and recall error on mock juror decision-making. *Legal and Criminological Psychology*, *19*, 332–348. https://doi.org/10.1111/lcrp.12001

Burrell, L. V., Johnson, M. S., & Melinder, A. (2016). Children as earwitnesses: Memory for emotional auditory events. *Applied Cognitive Psychology*, *30*(3), 323–331. https://doi.org/10.1002/acp.3202

Busby Grant, J. B., & Suddendorf, T. (2009). Preschoolers begin to differentiate the times of events from throughout the lifespan. *European Journal of Developmental Psychology*, *6*, 746–762. https://doi.org/10.1080/17405620802102947

Butler, S., Gross, J., & Hayne, H. (1995). The effect of drawing on memory performance in young children. *Developmental Psychology*, *31*, 597–608. https://doi.org/10.1037/0012-1649.31.4.597

Ceci, S. J., & Bruck, M. (1993). Suggestibility of the child witness: A historical review and synthesis. *Psychological Bulletin*, *113*, 403–439. https://doi.org/10.1037/0033-2909.113.3.403

Chae, Y., & Ceci, S. J. (2005). Individual differences in children's recall and suggestibility: The effect of intelligence, temperament and self-perceptions. *Applied Cognitive Psychology*, *19*(4), 383–407. https://doi.org/10.1002/acp.1094

Chae, Y., Goodman, G. S., Larson, R. P. et al. (2014). Children's memory and suggestibility about a distressing event: The role of children's and parent's attachment. *Journal of Experimental Child Psychology*, *123*, 90–111. https://doi.org/10.1016/j.jecp.2014.01.005 0022-0965/2014

Cordon, I. M., Silberkleit, G., & Goodman, G. S. (2016). Getting to know you: Familiarity, stereotypes, and children's eyewitness testimony. *Behavioral Sciences and the Law*, *34*, 74–94. https://doi.org/10.1002/bsl.2233

Crossman, A. M., & Lewis, M. (2006). Adults' ability to detect children's lying. *Behavioral Sciences & the Law*, *24*(5), 703–715. https://doi.org/10.1002/bsl.731

Cycowicz, Y. M., Friedman, D., Snodgrass, J. G., & Duff, M. (2001). Recognition and source memory for pictures in children and adults. *Neuropsychologia*, *39*, 255–267. https://doi.org/10.1016/S0028-3932(00)00108-1

Deese, J. (1959). Influence of inter-item associative strength upon immediate free recall. *Psychological Reports*, *5*(3), 305–312. https://doi.org/10.2466/pr0.1959.5.3.305

Deker, L., & Pathman, T. (2021). Did I visit the polar bear before the giraffe? Examining memory for temporal order and the temporal distance effect in early to middle childhood. *Applied Cognitive Psychology, 35,* 785–794. https://doi.org/10.1002/acp.3804

Dunn, L. M., & Dunn, L. M. (1981). *Peabody picture vocabulary test – revised.* American Guidance Service.

Faller, K. C. (2005). Anatomical dolls: Their use in assessment of children who may have been sexually abused. *Journal of Child Sexual Abuse, 14,* 1–21. https://doi.org/10.1300/J070v14n03_01

Finkelhor, D., Ormrod, R., Turner, H., & Hamby, S. L. (2005). The victimization of children and youth: A comprehensive, national survey. *Child Maltreatment, 10,* 5–25. https://doi.org/10.1177/1077559504271287

Fitzley, V. H., Okanda, M., Itakura, S., & Lee, K. (2011). Children's responses to yes-no questions. In M. Siegel & L. Surian (Eds.), *Access to language and cognitive development* (pp. 83–99). Oxford University Press.

Fivush, R. (in press). *Autobiographical memory and narrative in childhood.* In M. H. Bornstein, *Cambridge elements in child development.* Cambridge University Press

Fivush, R., Hudson, J., & Nelson, K. (1984). Children's long-term memory for a novel event: An exploratory study. *Merrill-Palmer Quarterly, 30,* 303–316. www.jstor.org/stable/23086104

Fonn, E. J., Zahl, J. H., & Tomsen, L. (2022). The boss is not always right: Norwegian preschoolers do not selectively endorse the testimony of a novel dominant agent. *Child Development,* 1–14. https://doi.org/10.1111/cdev.13722

Frawley-O'Dea, M. G., & Goldner, V. (2007). *Predatory priests, silenced victims: The sexual abuse crisis and the Catholic church.* Taylor & Francis.

Friedman, W. J. (1992). Children's time memory: The development of a differentiated past. *Cognitive Development, 7*(2), 171–187. https://doi.org/10.1016/0885-2014(92)90010-O

Friedman, W. J. (1993). Memory for the time of past events. *Psychological Bulletin, 113,* 44–66. https://doi.org/10.1037/0033-2909.113.1.44

Friedman, W. J. (2014). Development of memory for the times of past events. In P. J. Bauer & R. Fivush (Eds.), *The Wiley handbook on the development of children's memory* (pp. 394–407). Wiley-Blackwell.

Friedman, W. J., Gardner, A. G., & Zubin, N. R. E. (1995). Children's comparisons of the recency of two events from the past year. *Child Development, 66,* 970–983. https://doi.org/10.2307/1131792

Friedman, W. J., & Lyon, T. D. (2005). Development of temporal-reconstructive abilities. *Child Development, 76,* 1202–1216. https://doi.org/10.1111/j.1467-8624.2005.00844.x-i1

Gao, X., & Maurer, D. (2010). A happy story: Developmental changes in children's sensitivity to facial expressions of varying intensities. *Journal of*

Experimental Child Psychology, 107, 67–86. https://doi.org/10.1016/j.jecp.2010.05.003

Gardner, E., Gross, J., & Hayne, H. (2020). The effect of drawing and socioeconomic status on children's reports of a past experience. *Journal of Experimental Psychology: Applied, 26,* 397–410. https://doi.org/10.1037/xap0000264

Garon, N., Bryson, S. E., & Smith, I. M. (2008). Executive function in preschoolers: A review using an integrative framework. *Psychological Bulletin, 134,* 31–60. https://doi.org/10.1037/0033-2909.134.1.31

Gervais, J., Tremblay, R. E., Desmarais-Gervais, L., & Vitaro, F. (2000). Children's persistent lying, gender differences, and disruptive behaviours: A longitudinal perspective. *International Journal of Behavioral Development, 24,* 213–221. www.tandf.co.uk/journals/pp/01650254.html

Goodman, G. S., Golding, J. M., Helgeson, V. S., Haith, M. M., & Michelli, J. (1987). When a child takes the stand: Jurors' perceptions of children's eyewitness testimony. *Law and Human Behavior, 11,* 27–40. https://doi.org/10.1007/BF01044837

Goodman, G. S., Quas, J. A., Goldbarb, D., Gonzalves, L., & Gonzalez, A. (2019). Trauma and long-term memory for childhood events: Impact matters. *Child Development Perspectives, 13,* 3–9. https://doi.org/10.1111/cdep.12307

Gosse, L. L., & Roberts, K. P. (2014). Children's use of a "time line" to indicate when events occurred. *Journal of Police and Criminal Psychology, 29*(1), 36–43. https://doi.org/10.1007/s11896-013-9118-x

Gross, J., & Hayne, H. (1999). Drawing facilitates children's verbal reports after long delays. *Journal of Experimental Psychology: Applied, 5,* 265–283. https://doi.org/10.1037/1076-898X.5.3.265

Gunnar, M. R., Doom, J. R., & Esposito, E. A. (2015). Psychoneuroendocrinology of stress: Normative development and individual differences. In M. E. Lamb & R. M. Lerner (Eds.), *Handbook of child psychology and developmental science: Socioemotional processes* (7th ed., Vol. 3, pp. 106–151). Wiley.

Harris, P. L., & Gross, D. (1988). Children's understanding of real and apparent emotion. In J. W. Astington, P. L. Harris & D. R. Olson (Eds.), *Developing theories of mind* (pp. 295–314). Cambridge University Press.

Hayes, D. S., & Casey, D. M. (1992). Young children and television: The retention of emotional reactions. *Child Development, 63,* 1423–1436. https://doi.org/10.2307/1131566

Hayne, H., & Imuta, K. (2011). Episodic memory in 3- and 4-year-old children. *Developmental Psychobiology, 53,* 317–322. https://doi.org/10.1002/dev.20527

Hedrick, A. M., Haden, C. A., & Ornstein, P. A. (2009). Elaborative talk during and after an event: Conversational style influences children's memory reports. *Journal of Cognition and Development, 10,* 188–209. https://doi .org/10.1080/15248370903155841

Holcomb, M. J., & Jacquin, K. M. (2007). Juror perceptions of child eyewitness testimony in a sexual abuse trial. *Journal of Child Sexual Abuse, 16,* 79–95. https://doi.org/10.1300/J070v16n02_05

Holmes, P., & Farnfield, S. (2014). *The Routledge handbook of attachment: Implications and interventions.* Routledge/Taylor & Francis.

Howe, M. L. (2015). Memory development. In L. S. Liben, U. Muller & R. M. Lerner (Eds.), *Handbook of child psychology and developmental science: Cognitive processes* (7th ed., Vol. 2, pp. 203–249). Wiley.

Howe, M. L., Candel, I., Otgaar, H., Malone, C., & Wimmer, M. C. (2010). Valence and the development of immediate and long-term false memory illusions. *Memory, 18,* 58–75. https://doi.org/10.1080/09658210903476514

Howe, M. L., & Wilkinson, S. (2011). Using story contexts to bias children's true and false memories. *Journal of Experimental Child Psychology, 108*(1), 77–95. https://doi.org/10.1016/j.jecp.2010.06.009

Hughes, C., & Devine, R. T. (2015). A social perspective of theory of mind. In *Handbook of child psychology and developmental science,* edited by M. E. Lamb and R. M. Lerner (Vol. 3, pp. 564–609). Wiley.

Hughes, M., & Grieve, R. (1980). On asking children bizarre questions. *First Language, 1,* 149–160.

Johnson, M. K., Hashtroudi, S., & Lindsay, D. S. (1993). Source monitoring. *Psychological Bulletin, 114,* 3–28. https://doi.org/10.1037/0033-2909.114.1.3

Jones, T. M., Bottoms, B. L., & Stevenson, M. C. (2020). Child victim empathy mediates the influence of jurors' sexual abuse experiences on child sexual abuse case judgments: Meta-analyses. *Psychology, Public Policy, and Law, 26,* 312–332. https://doi.org/10.1037/law0000231

Karni-Visel, Y., Hirshkowitz, I., Lamb, M. E., & Blasbalg, U. (2019). Facilitating the expression of emotions by alleged victims of child abuse during investigative interviews using the revised NICHD protocol. *Child Maltreatment, 24,* 310–318. https://doi.org/10.1177/1077559519831382

Karpinski, A. C., & Scullin, M. H. (2009). Suggestibility under pressure: Theory of mind, executive function, and suggestibility in preschoolers. *Journal of Applied Developmental Psychology, 30,* 749–763. https://doi .org/10.1016/j.appdev.2009.05.004

Klemfuss, J. Z. (2015). Differential contributions of language skills to children's episodic recall. *Journal of Cognition and Development, 16,* 608–620. https://doi.org/10.1080/15248372.2014.952415

Klemfuss, J. Z., & Wang, Q. (2017). Narrative skills, gender, culture, and children's long-term memory accuracy of a staged event. *Journal of Cognition and Development, 18*, 577–594. https://doi.org/10.1080/ 15248372.2017.1392308

Krähenbühl, S., Blades, M., & Eiser, C. (2009). The effect of repeated questioning on children's accuracy and consistency in eyewitness testimony. *Legal and Criminological Psychology, 14*, 263–278. https://doi.org/ 10.1348/135532508X398549

Krettenauer, T., Colastante, T., Buchmann, M., & Malti, T. (2014). The development of moral emotions and decision-making from adolescence to early adulthood: A 6-year longitudinal study. *Journal of Youth Adolescence, 43*, 583–596. https://doi.org/10.1007/s10964-013-9994-5

Kulkofsky, S. (2010). The effect of verbal labels and vocabulary skill on memory and suggestibility. *Journal of Applied Developmental Psychology, 31*, 460–466. https://doi.org/10.1016/j.appdev.2010.09.002

Kulkofsky, S., Principe, G. F., Debaran, F. B., & Stouch, A. (2011). Just the facts or just for fun? Children's understanding of and sensitivity to retelling contexts. *Applied Cognitive Psychology, 25*, 727–738. https://doi.org/ 10.1002/acp.1744

LaBar, K. S., & Cabeza, R. (2006). Cognitive neuroscience of emotional memory. *Nature Reviews Neuroscience, 7*, 54–64. https://doi.org/10.1038/ nrn1825

Lamb, M. E., Orbach, Y., Hershkowitz, I., Esplin, P. W., & Hershkowitz, D. (2007a). A structured forensic interview protocol improves the quality of informativeness of investigative interviews with children: A review of research using the NICHD Investigative Interview Protocol. *Child Abuse and Neglect, 31*, 1201–1231. https://doi.org/10.1016/j.chiabu.2007.03.021

Lamb, M. E., Orbach, Y., Warren, A. R., Esplin, P. W., & Hershkowitz, I. (2007b). Enhancing performance: Factors affecting the informativeness of young witnesses. In M. P. Toglia, J. D. Read, D. F. Ross & R. C. L. Lindsay (Eds.), *Handbook of witness psychology* (pp. 429–451). Erlbaum.

Leventon, J. S., Stevens, J. S., & Bauer, P. J. (2014). Development in the neurophysiology of emotion process and memory in school-age children. *Developmental Cognitive Neuroscience, 10*, 21–33. http://creativecommons .org/licenses/by-nc-nd/3.0/

Loftus, E. F. (1979). *Eyewitness testimony.* Harvard University Press.

Loftus, E. F. (2019). Eyewitness testimony. *Applied Cognitive Psychology, 33*, 498–503. https://doi.org/10.1002/acp.3542

Loftus, E. F., & Palmer, J. C. (1974). Reconstruction of automobile destruction: Example of the interaction between language and memory. *Journal of Verbal*

Learning and Behavior, 13, 585–589. https://doi.org/10.1016/S0022-5371 (74)80011-3

Lowenstein, J. A., Blank, H., & Sauer, J. D. (2010). Uniforms affect the accuracy of children's eyewitness identification decisions. *Journal of Investigative Psychology and Offender Profiling, 7*, 59–73. https://doi.org/10.1002/jip.104

Mascaro, O., & Sperber, D. (2009). The moral, epistemic, and mindreading components of children's vigilance towards deception. *Cognition, 112*(3), 367–380. https://doi.org/10.1016/j.cognition.2009.05.012

McCauley, M. R., & Parker, J. F. (2001). When will a child be believed? The impact of victim's age and juror's gender on children's credibility and verdict in a sexual-abuse case. *Child Abuse and Neglect, 25*, 523–539. https://doi.org/10.1016/S0145-2134(01)00224-1

McGuire, K., London, K., & Wright, D. (2015). Developmental trends in false memory across adolescence and young adulthood: A comparison of DRM and memory conformity paradigms. *Applied Cognitive Psychology, 29*, 334–344. https://doi.org/10.1002/acp.3114

Meinhardt-Injac, B., Daum, M. M., & Meinhardt, G. (2020). Theory of mind development from adolescence to adulthood: Testing the two-component model. *British Journal of Developmental Psychology, 38*(2), 289–303. https://doi.org/10.1111/bjdp.12320

Melinder, A., Goodman, G. S., Eilertsen, D. E., & Magnussen, S. (2004). Beliefs about child witnesses: A survey of professionals. *Psychology, Crime & Law, 10*(4), 347–365. https://doi.org/10.1080/1068316031000161871

Miller, G. A. (1956). The magical number seven, plus or minus two: Some limits on our capacity for processing information. *Psychological Review, 63*, 81–97. https://doi.org/10.1037/0033-295X.101.2.343

Miller, P. H. (2002). *Theories of developmental psychology* (4th ed.). Worth.

Mitchell, K. J., Johnson, M. K., & Mather, M. (2003). Source monitoring and suggestibility to misinformation: Adult age-related differences. *Applied Cognitive Psychology, 17*, 107–119. https://doi.org/10.1002/acp.857

Mondloch, C. J., Geldart, S., Maurer, D., & Grand, R. L. (2003). Developmental changes in face processing skills. *Journal of Experimental Child Psychology, 86*, 67–84. https://doi.org/10.1016/S0022-0965(03)00102-4

Muller, U., & Kerns, K. (2015). The development of executive function. In L. S. Liben, U. Muller & R. M. Lerner (Eds.), *Handbook of child psychology and developmental science: Cognitive processes* (7th ed., Vol. 2, pp. 571–623). Wiley.

Newcombe, N. S., Balcomb, F., Ferrara, K., Hansen, M., & Koski, J. (2014). Two rooms, two representations? Episodic-like memory in toddlers and preschoolers. *Developmental Science, 17*, 743–756. https://doi.org/10.1111/desc.12162

Ngo, C. T., Alm, K. H., Metoki, A. et al. (2017). White matter structural connectivity and episodic memory in early childhood. *Developmental Cognitive Neuroscience, 28*, 41–53. https://doi.org/10.1016/j.dcn.2017.11.001

Nikonova, O., & Ogloff, J. R. P. (2005). Mock jurors' perceptions of child witnesses: The impact of judicial warning. *Canadian Journal of Behavioural Science/Revue Canadienne Des Sciences Du Comportement, 37*(1), 1–19. https://doi.org/10.1037/h0087241

Nordt, M., & Weigelt, S. (2017). Face recognition is similarly affected by viewpoint in school-aged children and adults. *PeerJ* 5:e3253. https://doi.org/10.7717/peerj.3253

Nunez, N., Kehn, A., & Wright, D. B. (2011). When children are witnesses: The effects of context, age and gender on adults' perceptions of cognitive ability and honesty. *Applied Cognitive Psychology, 25*, 460–468. https://doi.org/10.1002/acp.1713

Nysse-Carris, K. L., Bottoms, B. L., & Salerno, J. M. (2011). Experts' and novices' abilities to detect children's high-stakes lies of omission. *Psychology, Public Policy, and Law, 17*, 76–98. https://doi.org/10.1037/a0022136

Okanda, M., & Itakura, S. (2010). When do children exhibit a "Yes" bias? *Child Development, 81*(2), 568–580. https://doi-org.colby.idm.oclc.org/10.1111/j.1467-8624.2009.01416.x

Okanda, M., Kanda, T., Ishiguro, H., & Itakura, S. (2013). Three- and 4-year-old children's response tendencies to various interviewers. *Journal of Experimental Child Psychology, 116*, 68–77. https://doi.org/10.1016/j.jecp.2013.03.012

Okanda, M., Zhou, Y., Kanda, T., Ishiguro, H., & Itakura, S. (2018). I hear your yes-no questions: Children's response tendencies to a humanoid robot. *Infant and Child Development, 27*, 1–9. https://doi.org/10.1002/icd.2079

Ornstein, P. A., Baker-Ward, L., Gordon, B. N. et al. (2006). The influence of prior knowledge and repeated questioning on children's long-term retention of the details of a pediatric examination. *Developmental Psychology, 42*, 332–344. https://doi.org/10.1037/0012-1649.42.2.332

Otgaar, H., de Ruiter, C., Sumampouw, N., Erens, B., & Muris, P. (2021). Protecting against misinformation: Examining the effect of empirically based investigative interviewing on misinformation reporting. *Journal of Police and Criminal Psychology*, 36, 758–768.https://doi.org/10.1007/s11896-020-09401-2

Otgaar, H., van Ansem, R., Pauw, C., & Horselenberg, R. (2016). Improving children's interviewing methods? The effects of drawing and practice on children's memories for an event. *Journal of Police and Criminal Psychology, 31*, 279–287. https://doi.org/10.1007/s11896-016-9190-0

Pathman, T., Doydum, A., & Bauer, P. J. (2013). Bringing order to life events: Memory for the temporal order of autobiographical events over an extended period in school-aged children and adults. *Journal of Experimental Child Psychology, 115*, 309–325. https://doi.org/10.1016/j.jecp.2013.01.011

Pathman, T., & Ghetti, S. (2014). The eyes know time: A novel paradigm to reveal the development of temporal memory. *Child Development, 85*, 792–807. https://doi.org/10.1111/cdev.12152

Pathman, T., Larkina, M., Burch, M. M., & Bauer, P. J. (2013). Young children's memories for the times of personal past events. *Journal of Cognition and Development, 14*, 120–140. https://doi.org/10.1080/15248372.2011.641185

Peterson, C. (2015). A decade later: Adolescents' memory for medical emergencies. *Applied Cognitive Development, 29*, 826–834. https://doi.org/10.1002/acp.3192

Peterson, C., Sales, J. M., Rees, M., & Fivush, R. (2007). Parent-child talk and children's memory for stressful events. *Applied Cognitive Psychology, 21*, 1057–1075. https://doi.org/10.1002/acp.1314

Picard, L., Cousin, S., Guillery-Girard, B., Eustache, F., & Piolino, P. (2012). How do the different components of episodic memory develop? Role of executive functions and short-term feature-binding abilities. *Child Development, 83*, 1037–1050. https://doi.org/10.1111/j.1467-8624.2012.01736.x

Pillemer, D. B., Picariello, M. L., & Pruett, J. C. (1994). Very long-term memories of a salient preschool event. *Applied Cognitive Psychology, 8*, 95–106. https://doi.org/10.1002/acp.2350080202

Pollak, S. D., & Kistler, D. J. (2002). Early experience is associated with the development of early categorical representations for facial expressions of emotion. *Proceedings of the National Academy of Sciences, 99*, 9072–9076. www.pnas.org_cgi_doi_10.1073_pnas.142165999

Pons, F., Harris, P. L., & Rosnay, M. (2004). Emotion comprehension between 3 and 11 years: Developmental periods and hierarchical organization. *European Journal of Developmental Psychology, 1*(2), 127–152. https://doi.org/10.1080/17405620344000022

Poole, D. A., & Bruck, M. (2012). Divining testimony? The impact of interviewing props on children's reports of touching. *Developmental Review, 32*, 165–180. https://doi.org/10.1016/j.dr.2012.06.007

Poole, D. A., & Lindsay, D. S. (1995). Interviewing preschoolers: Effects of nonsuggestive techniques, parental coaching, and leading questions on reports of nonexperienced events. *Journal of Experimental Child Psychology, 60*, 129–154. https://doi.org/10.1006/jecp.1995.1035

Powell, M. B., Roberts, K. P., & Guadagno, B. (2007). Particularisation of child abuse offences: Common problems when questioning child witnesses. *Current Issues in Criminal Justice, 19*, 64–74. http://hdl.handle.net/10536/DRO/DU:30007276

Principe, G. F., Ornstein, P. A., Baker-Ward, L., & Gordon, B. N. (2000). The effects of intervening experiences on children's memory for a physical examination. *Applied Cognitive Psychology, 14*, 59–80. https://doi.org/10.1002/(SICI)1099-0720(200001)14:1<59::AID-ACP637>3.0.CO;2-4

Principe, G. F., Trumbull, J., Gardner, G., Van Horn, E., & Dean, A. M. (2017). The role of maternal elaborative structure and control in children's memory and suggestibility for a past event. *Journal of Experimental Child Psychology, 163*, 15–31. https://doi.org/10.1016/j.jecp.2017.06.001

Quas, J. A., Goodman, G. S., Bidrose, S. et al. (1999). Emotion and memory: Children's long-term remembering, forgetting, and suggestibility. *Journal of Experimental Child Psychology, 72*, 235–270. https://doi.org/10.1006/jecp.1999.2491

Ratner, H. H., Foley, M. A., & Gimpert, N. (2002). The role of collaborative planning in children's source monitoring errors and learning. *Journal of Experimental Child Psychology, 81*, 44–73. https://doi.org/10.1006/jecp.2001.2643

Roberts, K. P., Brubacher, S. P., Drohan-Jennings, D. et al. (2015). Developmental differences in the ability to provide temporal information about repeated events. *Applied Cognitive Psychology, 29*, 407–417. https://doi.org/10.1002/acp.3118

Roediger, H. L., & Butler, A. C. (2011). The critical role of retrieval practice in long-term retention. *Trends in Cognitive Sciences, 15*, 20–27. https://doi.org/10.1016/j.tics.2010.09.003

Roediger, H. L., & Karpicke, J. D. (2006). Test-enhanced learning: Taking memory tests improves long-term retention. *Psychological Science, 17*, 249–255. https://doi.org/10.1111/j.1467-9280.2006.01693.x

Roediger, H. L., & McDermott, K. B. (1995). Creating false memories: Remembering words not presented in lists. *Journal of Experimental Psychology: Learning, Memory, and Cognition, 21*(4), 803. https://doi.org/10.1037/0278-7393.21.4.803

Rogoff, B. (2014). Learning by observing and pitching in to family and community endeavors: An orientation. *Human Development, 57*, 69–81. https://doi.org/10.1159/000356757

Salmon, K., & Reese, E. (2015). Talking (or not talking) about the past: The influence of parent-child conversations about negative experiences on children's memories. *Applied Cognitive Psychology, 29*, 791–801. https://doi.org/10.1002/acp.3186

Scarf, D., Bode, H., Labuschagne, L. G., Gross, J., & Hayne, H. (2017). "What" and "where" was when? Memory for the temporal order of episodic events in children. *Developmental Psychobiology, 59*, 1039–1045. https://doi.org/10.1002/dev.21553

Scullin, M. H., & Ceci, S. J. (2001). A suggestibility scale for children. *Personality and Individual Differences, 30*, 843–856. https://doi.org/10.1016/S0191-8869(00)00077-5

Sheahan, C. L., Pica, E., & Puzzulo, J. D. (2021). Abuse is abuse: The influence of type of abuse, victim age, and defendant age on juror decision making. *Journal of Interpersonal Violence, 36*, 938–956. https://doi.org/10.1177/0886260517731316

Sluzenski, J., Newcombe, N. S., & Kovacs, S. L. (2006). Binding, relational memory, and recall of naturalistic events: A developmental perspective. *Journal of Experimental Psychology: Learning, Memory and Cognition, 32*, 89–100. https://doi.org/10.1037/0278-7393.32.1.89

Smetana, J. G., & Ball, C. L. (2018). Young children's moral judgments, justifications, and emotion attributions in peer relationship contexts. *Child Development, 89*(6), 2245–2263. https://doi.org/10.1111/cdev.12846

Spring, T., Saltzstein, H. D., & Peach, R. (2013). Children's eyewitness identification as implicit moral decision-making. *Applied Cognitive Psychology, 27*(2), 139–149. https://doi.org/10.1002/acp.2871

Steblay, N., Dysart, J., Fulero, S., & Lindsay, R. C. L. (2001). Eyewitness accuracy rates in sequential and simultaneous lineup presentations: A meta-analytic comparison. *Law and Human Behavior, 25*(5), 459–473. https://doi.org/10.1023/a:1012888715007

Sutherland, R., Pipe, M.-E., Schick, K., Murray, J., & Gobbo, C. (2003). Knowing in advance: The impact of prior event information on memory and event knowledge. *Journal of Experimental Child Psychology, 84*, 244–263. https://doi.org/10.1016/S0022-0965(03)00021-3

Szekely, E., Lucassen, N., Tiemeier, H. et al. (2014). Maternal depressive symptoms and sensitivity are related to young children's facial expression recognition: The Generation R Study. *Development and Psychopathology, 26*, 333–345. https://doi.org/10.1017/S0954579413001028

Talwar, V., Crossman, A., Williams, S., & Muir, S. (2011). Adult detection of children's selfish and polite lies: Experience matters. *Journal of Applied Social Psychology, 41*(12), 2837–2857. https://doi.org/10.1111/j.1559-1816.2011.00861.x

Talwar, V., Gordon, H. M., & Lee, K. (2007). Lying in the elementary school years: Verbal deception and its relation to second-order belief understanding. *Developmental Psychology*, *43*, 804–810. https://doi.org/10.1037/0012-1649.43.3.804

Talwar, V., Lavoie, J., & Grossman, A. M. (2019). Carving Pinocchio: Longitudinal examination of children's lying for different goals. *Journal of Experimental Child Psychology*, *181*, 34–55. https://doi.org/10.1016/j.jecp.2018.12.003 0022-0965/

Teoh, Y.-S., & Chang, T.-F. (2018). Comparing the effects of drawing and verbal recall techniques on children's memory accounts. *Scandinavian Journal of Psychology*, *59*, 631–633. https://doi.org/10.1111/sjop.12496

Tillman, K. A., & Barner, D. (2015). Learning the language of time: Children's acquisition of duration words. *Cognitive Psychology*, *78*, 57–77. https://doi.org/10.1016/j.cogpsych.2015.03.001

Tobey, A. E., & Goodman, G. S. (1992). Children's eyewitness memory: Effects of participation and forensic context. *Child Abuse and Neglect*, *16*, 779–796. https://doi.org/10.1016/0145-2134(92)90081-2

Uhl, E. R., Camilletti, C. R., Scullin, M. H., & Wood, J. M. (2016). Under pressure: Individual differences in children's suggestibility in response to intense social influence. *Social Development*, *25*(2), 422–434. https://doi.org/10.1111/sode.12156

Van Bergen, P., Wall, J., & Salmon, K. (2015). The good, the bad, and the neutral: The influence of emotional valence on young children's recall. *Journal of Applied Research in Memory and Cognition*, *4*, 29–35. https://doi.org/10.1016/j.jarmac.2014.11.001

Van de Kaap-Deeder, J., Soenens, B., Moratidis, A. et al. (2020). Towards a detailed understanding of preschool children's memory-related functioning and emotion regulation: The role of parents' observed reminiscence style, memory valence, and parental gender. *Developmental Psychology*, *56*, 1696–1708. https://doi.org/10.1037/dev0001048

Van de Vondervoort, J. W., & Hamlin, J. K. (2017). Preschoolers' social and moral judgments of third-party helpers and hinderers align with infants' social evaluations. *Journal of Experimental Child Psychology*, *164*, 136–151. https://doi.org/10.1016/j.jecp.2017.07.004

Voogt, A., & Klettke, B. (2017). The effect of gender on perceptions of credibility in child sexual assault cases: A systematic review. *Journal of Child Sexual Abuse*, *26*, 195–212. https://doi.org/10.1080/10538712.2017.1280576

Voogt, A., Klettke, B., & Crossman, A. (2019). Measurement of victim credibility in child sexual assault cases: A systematic review. *Trauma, Violence, & Abuse*, *20*, 51–66. https://doi.org/10.1177/1524838016683460

Voogt, A., Klettke, B., & Thomson, D. M. (2017). The development of a conceptual model of perceived victim credibility in child sexual assault cases. *Psychiatry, Psychology and Law, 24,* 760–769. https://doi.org/10.1080/13218719.2017.1315764

Voogt, A., Klettke, B., Thomson, D. M., & Crossman, A. (2020). The impact of extralegal factors on perceived credibility of child victims of sexual assault. *Psychology, Crime & Law, 26,* 823–848. https://doi.org/10.1080/1068316X.2020.1742336

Walter, J. L., & LaFreniere, P. J. (2007). Preschoolers' avoidance in a mishap paradigm: Implications of emotional adjustment, guilt, and shame. *North American Journal of Psychology, 9,* 111–130.

Wandry, L., Lyon, T. D., Quas, J. A., & Friedman, W. J. (2012). Maltreated children's ability to estimate temporal location and numerosity of placement changes and court visits. *Psychology, Public Policy, and the Law, 18,* 79–104. https://doi.org/10.1037/a0024812

Want, S. C., Pascalis, O., Coleman, M., & Blades, M. (2003). Recognizing people from the inner or outer parts of their faces: Developmental data concerning "unfamiliar" faces. *British Journal of Developmental Psychology, 21*(1), 125–135. https://doi.org/10.1348/026151003321164663

Watanabe, Y., & Lee, K. (2016). Children's motive for admitting to prosocial behavior. *Frontiers in Psychology, 7.* https://doaj.org/article/3641581559c74264a94331bca6cd0339

Waterman, A. H., & Blades, M. (2013). The effect of delay and individual differences on children's tendency to guess. *Developmental Psychology, 49,* 215–226. https://doi.org/10.1037/a0028354

Wellman, H. M. (2014). *Making minds: How theory of mind develops.* Oxford University Press.

Wright, D. B., Hanoteau, F., Parkinson, C., & Tatham, A. (2010). Perceptions about memory reliability and honesty for children of 3 to 18 years old. *Legal and Criminological Psychology, 15,* 195–207. https://doi.org/10.1348/135532508X400347

Zelazo, P. D., Frye, D., & Rapus, T. (1996). An age-related dissociation between knowing rules and using them. *Cognitive Development, 11,* 37–63. https://doi.org/10.1016/S0885-2014(96)90027-1

Zelazo, P. D., & Muller, U. (2011). Executive function in typical and atypical development. In U. Goswami (Ed.), *The Wiley-Blackwell handbook of childhood cognitive development* (2nd ed., pp. 574–603). Wiley-Blackwell.

Acknowledgments

I thank the many Colby College students who joined me in exploring children's event memory in courses and in the Colby Child Development Lab. This Element is a prime example of what is possible in a teacher-scholar context at a small liberal arts college. My student collaborators took the lead role in setting the agenda for our work by asking important and novel questions. I also thank T. Montgomery for technical support, two anonymous reviewers for their constructive comments on a previous draft, and the Clara C. Piper Endowed Professorship for financial support.

Cambridge Elements ☰

Child Development

Marc H. Bornstein

*Eunice Kennedy Shriver National Institute of Child Health
and Human Development, Bethesda*

Institute for Fiscal Studies, London

UNICEF, New York City

Marc H. Bornstein is an Affiliate of the *Eunice Kennedy Shriver* National Institute of Child Health and Human Development, an International Research Fellow at the Institute for Fiscal Studies (London), and UNICEF Senior Advisor for Research for ECD Parenting Programmes. Bornstein is President Emeritus of the Society for Research in Child Development, Editor Emeritus of *Child Development*, and founding Editor of *Parenting: Science and Practice.*

About the Series

Child development is a lively and engaging, yet serious and real-world subject of scientific study that encompasses myriad theories, methods, substantive areas, and applied concerns. Cambridge Elements in Child Development addresses many contemporary topics in child development with unique, comprehensive, and state-of-the-art treatments of principal issues, primary currents of thinking, original perspectives, and empirical contributions to understanding early human development.

Cambridge Elements ⁼

Child Development

Elements in the Series

Printed in the United States
by Baker & Taylor Publisher Services